GOD'S EXPECTATIONS
For
HIS DAUGHTERS

-a blunt conversation

SHARI PRICHARD

TABLE OF CONTENTS

Dedication

*T*his book is dedicated to my family. They are my encouragement and my heart.

To my husband, Mark, who knows me better than anyone and loves me anyway. I have witnessed the changes God has made in your heart over the years and in our home. You are my encourager, best friend and I thank you for the life we have together. We will never be perfect, but we will always love one another.

To my daughter, Nicole. I am blessed to witness the young woman God has designed you to be. I see His love and a passion in you. I also see your desire to share Him with the world and I am thankful. You are funny, smart, talented and just plain adorable. I wait with excited anticipation of what God will call you to in the future.

To my son Wesley, you make me smile everyday with your wit and appetite for Christ. It is hard to believe that such a cute little boy has grown into a remarkable, intelligent, and loving young man. I wait with eager expectancy as God's plan for your life unfolds.

To my daughter-in-law Megan, Jesus answered my prayers when He brought you into my son's life. You love him with pure transparency. Your kind heart and beautiful smile light up the room when you enter. You are an incredible Mother. Mark and I are blessed that you are part of our family.

Acknowledgements

*T*hanks for the support from my biological and spiritual families. Where would I be today without Crossroads Christian Church! Thanks to all of the remarkable women that have grown with me over the years–you mean more to me than words can express.

A special thank you to the Worship Team *Crossover* – you guys *"blow the roof off"* every Sunday morning. I love you all so much!

To Shelley, Lynette, Angela, Terry, and Nici–I thank God each day for your friendship. I am blessed to share this journey with women who love Jesus and want to share Him with the world.

To Cherie Metcalf, thank you for your encouragement and brilliant editing skills. You took my conversation to the next level. In addition, to Blue Heart Photography, I am so blessed that God connected us.

Introduction–Getting Started

*W*elcome to a blunt conversation about God designed specifically for women. Since you've chosen this book, you are probably looking for something that is missing in your life. Are you tired of the status quo? Do you feel like a zombie in life right now? Are you just dragging from one day until the next? You may be one of the millions of women out there who ask themselves, "Is this all life has for me?" That is exactly where I was several years ago, until I decided I was ready to travel down a new road. How about you? Are you ready?

This is a story of what God has taught me while trying to get to know Him. Looking back on this time in my life makes me smile now as I reflect on what a different person I am today. Your story will be different and unique. One incredible attribute of God is how He allows us to experience Him differently. While we all may have some similar stories, we will have many personal and intimate experiences with God designed just for us. Therefore, I pray that somewhere in these pages you will find encouragement and hope.

Making a life change is difficult at any age. I know because I have been experiencing changes for the past thirteen years. As it says in *Matthew 19:26, Jesus said, "With man this is impossible, but with God all things are possible."* As difficult as it may be, I know change is possible. I've personally experienced it and I've seen others experience transformation. I have witnessed the lost and broken find hope and peace. I have witnessed the addicted heal and the cheater repent.

We live in a society where we expect everything now. God's timing does not work that way. He has a plan and a purpose that often does not line up with our timeframe. This may be one of the toughest life lessons to learn, but we must let go of our time expectations and live in God's time not ours. Understanding God's timing will lead to true victory.

What exactly does it mean *to live in true victory*? It sounds unattainable, but living in victory is having peace within you and being able to rely on God for everything. There's another huge lesson: rely on God for everything. I can expound on this topic since my life has totally changed in the past 26 years. However, where do *you* start? Where are *you* in your walk with God? Maybe you are just starting, or maybe you're stuck somewhere in the middle? Do you have internal turmoil between a genuine spiritual commitment and worldly anchors holding you captive? I'm guessing you may be going through a struggle or just beginning to get to know God and that is why God brought you to this book. He wants us to encourage one another, especially when we struggle:

Romans 5:3-5 (NIV) Not only so, but we also rejoice in our sufferings because we know that suffering produces perseverance; perseverance, character; and character hope. And hope does not disappoint us, because God has poured out his love into our hearts by the Holy Spirit, whom He has given us.

When I first read this scripture, I thought, "Now there's a strange idea. God wants me to rejoice in my suffering?" It just didn't make sense until I stopped and studied it. This scripture resonated with me once I started to understand that He IS our strength, and in His strength, I could stand tall when life's torpedoes tried to blow me up.

I'm excited you are joining me on this journey. Together we will explore new territory that God wants to establish and grow in you. You'll find tons of Scripture in this book because the Bible is God speaking to us. The Bible gives us specific direction for our lives and is necessary in discovering God's expectations.

If you have never asked God to come into your heart and be your personal Lord and Savior, that's the first step. Ask God to forgive you of your sins. Ask Him to take up residence in your heart and acknowledge Him for dying on the cross and rising again. Next, find a good Bible preaching church and attend regularly. Don't let anyone or anything separate you from God and this spiritual journey. If you don't have a Bible get one, it's your roadmap for this journey.

I am praying for everyone who will ever read this book while I am writing it. I know God will change your life forever. He surely continues to change mine. Okay, let's get started.

Chapter 1

Surrender

*og hovering over the lake like a blanket of snow, yet the clarity of that morning will be seared in my memory forever. Two hawks frolicking in the sky revealed a peace I only dreamed of. This was the day the war ended, the battle was over, and I finally stopped fighting God and surrendered to Him. I was twenty-one years old, in college, married and working part-time as a waitress. God placed a young lady in my life at work who was a sold-out Christian. Her love for God was evident in her actions and her words. She told me that Jesus loved me more than I could imagine and I needed to accept Him. Shortly after graduation, on a warm May morning, I slowly walked out into the middle of a lake in Kentucky and surrendered myself to the Creator. That's where it all started for me.

Genesis 1:1 (NIV) "In the beginning God created the heavens and earth."

The "beginning" is that moment in time when God decided to create the earth. *We all* started here and everything that was to come followed. You need to start here. Understanding that what you are searching for is not about something created but about the Creator. As we explore what God wants from us we must first accept who He is.

First, we know God is the Creator. In the book of Genesis, we find the story of how God spoke the universe into existence and every living creature on it. Next, we see that God created man and placed him in the Garden of Eden. It was several verses later that God decided it was not good for man to be alone so He created Eve.

Genesis 2:22 (NIV) Then the Lord God made a woman from the rib he had taken out of the man, and he brought her to the man.

Ladies this is some important stuff. We were not created from man's feet to be his slave. God decided man needed a helper because it must have been evident that Adam was not going to be "good" alone. The female race was specifically designed with a purpose. From the beginning, God designed the structure for male and female relationships. I view this as the importance God then placed on the need for female existence. If man was complete, then God would have left it that way. But, we were needed. We were chosen into creation for an extremely important reason; helping the man. We will discuss this topic in detail later. For now just try to spend some time thinking about the Creator and reading the first couple of chapters in Genesis.

It is not about me...

Now that we understand who the Creator is, we can move forward. God however, is so much more than the Creator. He is the Father, Son and Holy Spirit. He is the one who knows you better than you will ever know yourself and loves you more than you can possibly imagine.

One of the hardest lessons for many of us is to learn is that living a Christian life is not about us. What it boils down to is guiding others to Jesus. That is exactly what my friend did for me in college. She took me by the hand and led me straight to the only one who could ever really change my life. God is the beginning and the end. He is eternal. We were created to live in a relationship with Him. He is everything. That is who God is. We are eternal beings and Jesus died for every person you will ever meet. However, understanding the personality of God can be difficult at times.

My childhood memories consist of sitting on cold, wooden pews for three or more hours watching spit flying out of the red-faced Preachers' mouths and the words hell, damnation and fire being repeated over and over. My father was one of those Preachers, and at a young age, I found myself terrified of God. I knew He was real, but I spent my time fearing how I was going to screw up and be zapped by the Almighty. This distorted view of God followed me for years. The last time I regularly attended my father's church, the Preacher spent an hour hammering that women who cut their hair were living in sin, and they would pay the price someday. At the tender age of thirteen I thought, "This does not sound correct. Why would God care more about my hair than my heart?" I asked my father about it later that day over Sunday dinner and he reminded me that "a woman's hair is her glory," one of his favorite quotes and that was it. However, God would not let me go that easy. My seventh grade teacher invited me to her church. This church had a bus. For the next two years, it would come and pick me up on Sunday mornings. Looking back now, I can't believe I got away with that. But, I'm sure it was all part of God's plan. At my teacher's church, I was taught to memorize scripture, and I heard something strange for the first time. God loves me.

You are not in control...

Now, fast forward eight years later and again I heard this strange concept that the Creator loved me, and I needed to *surrender myself to God*. What did surrender myself to God mean? Basically, the Bible tells us we are to yield our will to God's will and put Him first. What would that look like in my life? We must submit to God's Word, (doing what it says) and trust God for all things in our lives: our money, our family, our health, everything. I was told to think about God as if I was the passenger on the flight of life and God was the pilot. I was confident in the pilot's ability to get me where I needed to go. He knew the route. He knew the estimated time of arrival. He is totally in control and I must have full confidence in His ability.

This is a hard concept for women who like control. I like control too. Yet, I've come to understand, no matter how much I want to control a situation; my course is NEVER the precise course God would take.

When I first started to talk through this concept, I was concerned I could not do it. What if I wasn't ready? What if I failed? What if? What if? Satan tried to convince me I was not good enough. Was this really how I was meant to live? How would my life change? What would I have to give up? Do any of these questions sound familiar?

I've been on this journey of discovering God's truth for twenty-six years now. When I started this journey let's just say my husband believed in the Lord, had been baptized but was not thrilled to be on a wild Jesus rollercoaster. For all of you out there with husbands who are not enthusiastic to learn more about Jesus, I totally understand. However, today my story is quite different.

In the beginning my thoughts swirled around activities, I would need to give up, like going out on the town with friends. I considered the party I was missing until I realized every night only led to a morning with a terrible headache and embarrassing memories I wish I could forget. Therefore, after some profound evaluating, I realized there really was not much to relinquish that made me happy or was good for me.

When you submit your life to God, you are making an agreement with Him to do things in His way, His time, His everything. That is exactly what He expects from us. I know, you're thinking this sounds like work. It is. As you practice daily submission to God, it no longer feels like work but just how you live. To begin, look at yourself in the mirror and be brutally honest. Do you like what you see? I didn't.

I was someone who would at least weekly, find myself discussing someone else's life and often making fun of it. Are gossip and slander attractive personality traits? This was one method I used to distance myself from people because I was not interested in developing close relationships with anyone. Why? Because people just hurt you and they can't be trusted, so why bother. Nice attitude, right? The actions I thought were keeping me safe were actually isolating me. After leaving college over the next twelve years I found myself without one close female friend, and no one that I could share stories of my kids, husband or this weird God thing with. This is actually where the enemy (satan) wants each one of us. The enemy wants us isolated and totally alone. This is not God's plan.

1 Peter 5:8 (NIV) Be self-controlled and alert. Your enemy the devil prowls around like a roaring lion looking for someone to devour.

Think about that scripture with me for just a moment. How does a lion devour his prey? He separates the weak from the pack. He isolates one from the safety of the herd, and he devours it. It is exactly the same with us today, Sister. The enemy would like nothing better than to keep us alone, weak, and completely isolated. We are vulnerable there. Suddenly, the safety of a pack sounds pretty good.

Falling in love with Jesus...

Just dream with me for a minute; you no longer have to worry about anything. He is in control of all aspects of your life and He loves you more than you can ever imagine. The peace you will experience while surrendering to God is unimaginable. Aren't you tired of working so hard to be in control of everything? I know I got to a point in my life where I was literally exhausted from worrying and stressing over every life detail all the time. Sound familiar? Let's look at some scripture for clear direction on submission.

James 4:7 (NIV) Submit yourself, then, to God. Resist the devil, and he will flee from you. Come near to God and he will come near to you.

Now get your Bible and read that verse again. Meditate on each word. Think about what it means to you, personally. It is specific direction on how to fall in love with Jesus. We are so blessed to serve a God who loves us enough to be specific with us. I need to visualize a new path before I take it, and what could be clearer? Come near to God and He will come near to you. I get so excited just thinking about that. Okay, so what do you draw from these passages regarding submission?

We are already submitted to something whether we are aware of it or not. This fact became clear to me when I was working as a manager at a local business. I always wanted to give 110% in every situation. However, I found myself being taken advantage of. Situations like racing to get my boss his afternoon tea so he would not be yelling my name down the hallway, or picking up food for my boss's kid on my lunch break and paying for it. I was totally submitted to my job. I was submitted to the workplace. I was trapped, and my life had to change.

First and foremost, God must become the most important entity in our lives. This happens as we get to know Him. We spend time with Him through prayer and Bible study and we find ourselves falling madly in love with the Creator. When I first heard the concept of *falling in love with Jesus* I thought the person talking to me must be intoxicated. I never thought of God that way. I thought it was about rules. Yes, God does call us to be obedient children but He wants a relationship. God loves us more than we can imagine – we are His creation.

The dreaded 'O' word...

Driving home in traffic while my brain bounced from one evening activity to the other was normal. The drive would only take about ten minutes but it was ten minutes of total stress because I knew waiting at home was a hungry family. By the time my car pulled in the driveway I was exhausted and frustrated. I had to start dinner with my business suite still on while the kids and my husband repeatedly told me how hungry they were. Sound like fun? In the refrigerator my best friend was waiting for me. She was dark red and sweet. While I cooked dinner I would drink at least two glasses and sometimes have a third with dinner. My stress seemed to slowly drift away. The fact I just dropped something on the floor became rather amusing. By the time dinner was on the table, I was smiling.

However, the Bible tells us to be of *little wine*. This is something I know many of us have struggled with which is why I think it is important to talk about. I believe to be of *little wine* does not mean drinking a bottle of wine each day. Don't get me wrong. I do not think it is sinful to have a glass of wine. However, if it is excessive then yes it is wrong.

I was not living the life that God was calling me to live. I was merely existing, trying to distract myself from the discontentment I harbored in my heart because my life was not what I thought it should be. My husband was not what I thought he should be, my job was difficult at best, my kids needed so much from me and I kept asking myself, "Is this really all there is?" The Creator did not create us to wallow in self.

When I first realized God required my obedience, I automatically stiffened. You see I was brought up in a strict legalistic home. Because the rules at the time seemed ridiculous, I could be rather rebellious. When I would think about being obedient to God at first, it rubbed me the wrong way. Yet, as I matured and came to the understanding Jesus wanted a love relationship with me, obedience became easier. Now I rejoice in obedience because I understand it, but that was not always the case.

Reading the Bible at times felt like a chore. It was not a chore I looked forward to but I knew it was good so I did it. One day my pastor said, "Shari, if you will read your Bible for fifteen minutes each day it will change your life." I thought to myself *that is so easy for you to say, you get paid to read your Bible all day. You don't have all of my responsibilities and problems*. Like I said earlier I was a tad rebellious. However, there was my catch phrase–*change your life*. God knows exactly how to get our attention. Trust me, I've tried every diet fad out there. I've tried every weird piece of exercise equipment, colon cleansing products, vitamins, herbs – you name it. If it claimed to *change your life* I was up for it. Of course, none of these things ever met my expectations.

One Monday morning I awoke with a determination to show my pastor he was wrong. I got up twenty minutes early, dragged myself to the coffee pot, waited patiently as the aroma of my new best friend filled the air, set a timer for fifteen minutes and started reading my Bible. Before I began, I prayed that God would help me to understand it and grow a love for it in my heart. I started in Matthew. It wasn't like I had never read it before, but this time I was actually studying it. Looking up clarifications and highlighting. I thought if I was going to take this challenge I needed to give some effort. For the next three months, five days per week this was my new routine. I could not believe there was so much I missed before. The Bible started to come alive for me, I looked forward to my fifteen minutes each morning.

I was starting to understand what God wanted from me; a relationship. The Bible was full of examples from Jesus' life of what a loving relationship looked like. At first it felt strange and foreign to me. Now it feels like home.

Using Jesus' life as our example, we have a clear description of what we should be striving for. I remember some days feeling as though I was never going to be good enough, but I kept going. I started to attend church every Sunday and going to women's Bible study. My new life began.

Slowly, day by day, I began to see small changes all around me. I began to feel a little bit different. My perspective about people and life situations slowly started to change. My heart was softening, my anger was decreasing and my desire to share Jesus with others was growing. I'll be bluntly honest. At first it was weird. However, I was determined no matter what happened, I would confess each day God is good, faithful and loves me more than I can ever imagine. A whole new world was unfolding before my very eyes.

Questions for thought…

1. What is holding you back from fully surrendering your-self to Jesus?

2. What are you afraid of giving up?

3. Are you willing to invest fifteen minutes per day in your eternity?

Action steps…

I understand for some of you, surrendering yourself to Jesus is a scary thought. The truth is, you are not giving up anything of real value, only receiving the best present you could ever imagine – eternity with Jesus. You may need to spend some time here and ask God to show you what you are missing. This is a life change and one you will never regret. Let go of control and accept the freedom that Jesus has to offer.

Chapter 2

Commit

he thought kept racing through my mind over and over. *Am I good enough, am I ready?* I would try to push the thought out of my mind, but it just kept returning. The Worship Leader at our church stood behind me one Sunday, heard me sing and asked if I would join the worship team. I said, "Okay," but I was petrified. The first Sunday as I stood in front of the congregation, I literally had to remove my contacts in order to maintain consciousness. As a teen I took voice lessons and sang in bars occasionally with a fake identification. Now standing in front of all of those people singing about a God I barely knew, I thought I would vomit.

I was just beginning to become comfortable with being one of the four singers on stage when the worship leader told me he was leaving town and if I did not take over his responsibilities, the church would not have worship. Every fiber of my being was screaming *NO*! I just stared at him with a lifeless glaze and then walked away. As an act of encouragement, the church leadership thought it would be a great idea to send me to a conference in order to learn more about worship. I agreed, but with hesitation and disgust.

I will never forget walking into the church at this conference. The sanctuary would easily seat thousands and thinking, "Seriously, this is all about Jesus?" That night was my first experience with authentic worship. I had never experienced a full band at a church or been part of a contemporary worship service. As the lights dimmed and only the soft candlelight filled the room, the leader began to pray for God to have His way and the music started. I just stood there at first and listened to the hearts of the worshippers who honestly wanted nothing more in that moment than to praise God. I closed my eyes and began to sing from my soul for the very first time. Tears streamed down my

29

face. I finally got it. This is what worship meant. In that moment, I wanted nothing more than to praise God and connect with Him.

The lightbulb went off. I was being called to draw people into the presence of God. I could hardly believe God wanted me. I had made so many mistakes and yet He seriously wanted *me*. After regaining my composure, I ran to the foyer and called my husband to tell him the good news. I knew God was calling me to be a Worship Leader. I didn't have all of the *how tos* answered, but I knew this was my calling. My husband listened in silence and then said, "Honey slow down, and they are trying to brain wash you. We will discuss this when you get home."

The truth...

The wonderful fact about God's love for us is that it is eternal, it never changes and He can never love us more or less than He does *at this exact moment*. This is truth. It doesn't matter where you've been or what you've been doing. God loves you today just as you are. God cannot love you more or less than He does in this exact moment. Just stop and think about this truth with me. He sees all of our mistakes and loves us anyway. His love is free and will NEVER change! He has "unlimited patience."

1 Timothy 1:15-16 (NIV) Here is a trustworthy saying that deserves full acceptance: Christ Jesus came into the world to save sinners – of whom I am the worst. However, for that very reason I was shown mercy so that in me, the worst of sinners, Christ Jesus might display his unlimited patience as an example for those who would believe on him and receive eternal life

Don't let a bad day make you feel as though you are not worthy. That is a lie from satan trying to fog your focus. We all make mistakes because we are human. God is aware of that fact. Pray, ask for forgiveness and start again. This cycle is one you will experience daily. In other words, you are going to sin. You will not be perfect until you enter Heaven. Maintain a positive attitude and keep repeating this scripture:

John 3:16 (NIV) *"For God so loved the world (insert your name for the world), He gave His one and only Son and whoever believes in Him shall not perish but have everlasting life."*

Life Worship...

Early in my spiritual makeover days, God used a common situation to get my attention. I found myself with a broken right wrist. Big deal, right? It was a big deal. I couldn't perform normal daily activities like brushing my hair, teeth, or dressing myself. I was depressed. I was now working at church as a part-time Worship Leader and beginning to understand the responsibility of the position. After having the cast on for three months, the doctor said I might need surgery and then back in the cast for another three months. Seriously? Half of a year in a cast?

Yet during this time, my life totally changed. I could no longer run away from God and I found myself needing Him more than ever before. While I was thrilled to use my voice for God, I felt broken and wounded. It was in those moments of feeling less than human, in a pit of pity, God continued to tell me He loved me and He was there. I was a miserable mess. Have you ever been there? A season when you just keep focusing on the negative?

I wallowed in my depression until I could no longer stand myself. I made a conscious decision to choose the light, and to run toward Him at full speed. I quit my dead-end job and opened my own consulting company; something I had wanted to do for years. Within a month, God was getting me up every morning with a head full of thoughts and conversations which became this book. I told God I was not a writer, and He told me to just sit down and write. Therefore, I did. God has a wonderful sense of humor.

During this time in my life I uttered one prayer every day. *"God, Your will be done in this situation. No matter the outcome, I know You love me and You are in charge."* It was so freeing to trust God.

God demonstrated His mercy, and no surgery was needed, only ten weeks of rehabilitation. The lesson I learned, I have re-played countless times in my mind. God listens and responds when His children are running toward Him. He holds out his hand when we are senseless and make wrong decisions. He doesn't leave us, He just loves us.

Our submission to God is a moment-by-moment experience. Stop and think about this with me. At any point during the day, we can make a right or wrong decision. Our actions and our words are either positive or negative. The key to success in this area is to train your brain *to stop and think, how would Jesus want me to handle this?* Each time you choose His ways, you are worshiping God with your life – *life worship*.

Romans 12:1-2 (NIV) Therefore, I urge you, brothers and sisters, in view of God's mercy, to offer your bodies as a living sacrifice, holy and pleasing to God—this is your true and proper worship. ² Do not conform to the pattern of this world, but be transformed by the renewing of your mind. Then you will be able to test and approve what God's will is—his good, pleasing and perfect will.

How you live your life each day is true worship. Earlier I was talking about singing to God, which is a form of worship, but what I am talking about now is more. It is making a conscious decision that nothing is more important than living your life as proof of this relationship. This is how we express to God our love for Him. Each decision you make either pulls you closer to God or pushes you further away. Every day, with every breath you have the opportunity to worship Jesus with your ordinary life. Take some time and allow this concept to absorb into your mind and then down into your heart. *Every decision you make is an opportunity to worship God.* At work, home, in the grocery store, in your relationships, be conscious of your actions and words because at the end of the day, what you did minute by minute, was your *life worship* to God.

Questions for thought...

1) Is there a lie the enemy has whispered to your heart, that you just can't shake? Write it down, recognize it for what it is, a lie, and ask God to give you clarity over the situation.

2) What keeps you from making good Godly decisions?

3) Do you know what your *life worship* looks like? Journal this week some of your *life worship* moments for strength and encouragement.

Action steps...

I find the most important step I take each day to ensure I am making Godly decisions is controlling my brain. I do this by listening to contemporary Christian music, watching positive movies and television shows, and memorizing some powerful scripture. It is easy to make a wrong choice; we must prepare to make right ones. Think about what you are thinking about and choose to focus on beauty, goodness, and be determined to do what is right according to God's Word.

Chapter 3

Pray

As strange as it may sound, my bathroom is my favorite prayer place. It is the one place where I can be alone with God and usually never interrupted. The walls are white with a pink and green dotted border just above the white and pink ceramic tile. My bathroom is girly, which is just the way I like it. In this room, I have had hundreds of conversations with Jesus. Here, He has heard me laugh, praise, cry, and scream. He has heard it all.

Prayer is a powerful tool. Through it, God can move mountains, repair broken hearts, heal the sick, and restore relationships. Prayer is a daily conversation, which grows our relationship with The Almighty. How do you grow a friendship with a person you just met? It is the same concept as growing our relationship with Jesus. God can't change us, unless we are willing. God cannot begin to transform us, unless our hearts and minds are open. Jesus can't become our best friend unless we spend time with Him.

Years ago, I prayed on my way to work after dropping off the kids at school. I thought this was adequate. I lived six miles from my place of work, so my prayer time was about two or three minutes each day. I assumed I was doing enough. At least I was consistent, I mean, I was praying *every* day.

How much time do you spend with the people you love? Do you spend at least two or three minutes per day with your family or your friends? Just think how your kids would respond if you only gave them two or three minutes each day. My sad little prayer time was always the same... "Thank you for all you do, protect my family, and bring us safely back together tonight." I prayed the same prayer every day, Monday through Friday. (I was off on Saturday and Sunday since I prayed at church). Can you imagine how sad God must have been every time I opened my mouth? I was completely missing the entire point of prayer.

What is *the point* you ask? The point is that prayer is our direct lifeline to the Creator of the universe. As we grow an intimate relationship with our Lord, we need to spend time with Him; talk to him daily for more than a couple of minutes. Share your fears, wants, disappointments, and desires with the Almighty. Think about it, you are talking to the One who placed all the stars in the sky!

Prayer is a special time when we can come before the Lord and praise Him for all He does in our lives. I think every woman in the world has at least one situation or person in her life to be thankful for. The Bible has some clear direction on the topic:

Philippians 4:6 (NIV) Do not be anxious about anything, but in everything, by prayer and petition, with thanksgiving, present your requests to God. And the peace of God, which transcends all understanding, will guard your hearts and your minds in Christ Jesus.

The first time this Scripture really came alive for me was when I was in my mid-twenties and Mark and I just welcomed our first child into the world. There is nothing like holding your baby for the first time and experiencing a love you never imagined. We took our son home and began a new routine. Our lives were changed forever, and we were so grateful.

Our son was less than a year old when my husband came home with his last paycheck from the job that had moved us during my pregnancy from one state to another. I was looking for work but was told repeatedly that I was *over qualified.* I finally found a tolerable job, paying twenty thousand dollars less than my last job, but we were desperate. My husband struggled with being laid off, and for the next several months, paying our normal bills became overwhelming. We had no other choice but to buy groceries on credit cards. During this time, I remembered what the young lady who walked me to salvation said, "Life will be tough, but God will never leave you." Looking back, I know it was the promise God gives us in Philippians 4:6. I was oddly peaceful. Each morning, I would get up, pray, and go to my little job, and I had peace. God was faithful. Within the year, we found new jobs back in the state where we had moved from. Our lives finally started to regain financial stability.

Truth in action...

One of the reasons I love Philippians 4:6 is because I have lived this scripture. Our Heavenly Father assures us everything is going to be fine. He promises us peace, not just a common peace, but a peace that *transcends all understanding*. What does God's peace look like? It is the mother whose child is critically ill in the hospital, and she chooses to hold onto Jesus, encouraging others by her strength. It is the woman with breast cancer who is in the middle of chemotherapy with a smile on her face because she has total trust in the Father's plan. It is the woman whose husband died, and she looks you in the eye and says, "It hurts, but I know God is still here." In every situation, there is calmness where there could be chaos. There is tranquility in the air where there could be confusion. This peace transcends all understanding. It doesn't make sense to the world watching, but other Christians understand it, recognize it, and are strengthened by it.

As I walked in spiritual growth, my prayer grew into "God your will and not mine." These six simple words have changed my life. The Bible tells us the prayers of the righteous are powerful and effective (James 5:16). Righteousness is identified as those who are trying to do what is right.

Mark 11:23-25 (NIV) "I tell you the truth, if anyone says to this mountain, "Go, throw yourself into the sea, and does not doubt in his heart but believes that what he says will happen, it will be done for him. Therefore I tell you, whatever you ask for in prayer, believe that you have received it, and it will be yours. And when you stand praying, if you hold anything against anyone, forgive him, so that your Father in heaven may forgive you your sins.

This Scripture tells us to believe we have received our prayer requests, and it will be ours. Do you pray in that manner? It is not a prideful attitude but rather humble strength when we pray, knowing that God will provide. I slowly began to put these Biblical principles to work in my life, and our Heavenly Father kept His promise – He changed my life.

Remember the story of how I started reading the Bible? Well, after six months, I was in a routine. During this time, God brought me one book after another that held a specific life lesson He needed me to learn. It was astonishing how each book I read said something specific about me and touched my heart. Don't get me wrong, I was still in my Bible every day, but I read tons of other books from female Christian authors that painted the picture of what living a Christian life looked like. I found direct *how tos* for me in these books. Each day I was amazed and touched to think that the One who created all was speaking directly to me. Little old selfish me was finally beginning to understand the only way to be content in life was serving God.

Stepping into my calling...

Earlier, I wrote about my first experience with authentic worship. I returned to my church and as my journey with God continued, He made it extremely clear to me that He was calling me to be a Worship Leader. I slowly started to understand what the position required.

The church building was previously a sports gym. The concrete floor and high ceilings were not conducive to live music. The stage lights, which were a first for our church, indicated that this specific Sunday was going to be different. I prayed that morning that the Holy Spirit would open my eyes to the unseen and allow me a glimpse of heaven. Some may say it was bold to ask, but for me it was how my relationship with my Heavenly Father was growing.

For the first time, when I stepped on stage, I was not afraid. I was not shaken, and my contacts were still in place. As the music started and the lights dimmed, I opened my mouth and found a freedom I had never experienced before. There was a strength I had never experienced before, and I was tingling all over. As I looked to the ceiling rafters in the back of the room, I could see the gates were opened and the angels were rejoicing as we praised God. It blew me away! I had found my calling. I was exactly where the Almighty designed me to be, leading others into the presence of our Savior so they could connect with Him. It was not about me, it was about undertaking the job He designed for me–leading others to Him.

I now understand what an amazing opportunity it is to lead people into His presence. This is an area only He can call you. It is not an occupation men can assign. Now, when I stand on stage in front of our congregation of four hundred or more, there is nothing more exciting than to see people worshiping our Savior. Over the past ten years, I have witnessed hundreds of lives surrendered to Jesus during our worship service, and there is absolutely nothing better! I later found out, ten people every day for almost a year prayed my stubborn heart into submission. I am so thankful.

Psalm 89:1 (NIV) I will sing of the Lord's great love forever; with my mouth I will make your faithfulness known through all generations.

Questions for thought...

1) How much time do you spend each day in prayer?

2) Do you find it hard to pray?

3) What are you being called to do?

Action steps...

First, understand that praying is simply talking to Jesus. It is a conversation, where the other person never grows tired of listening to you. There is nothing you can tell God that He doesn't already know so complete honestly is a must. Don't be ashamed or afraid. God loves you and He wants to hear from you.

Chapter 4

Submit

—·≻- ❧♥❧ -≺·—

*H*ave you ever used your tongue as a dagger? Maybe a loaded pistol? I have. I can definitely relate to those of you, who during times of war, have broken out the big guns.

The topic of submitting to your husband deserves a chapter all to itself, maybe an entire book. I know from personal experience, if this is a new concept, it can take years to implement. However, once you initiate Godly submission in your home, the environment will change. You will change. If you are not married, you may gain a little insight, too. Let's get started.

1 Peter 3:1-2 (NIV) Wives, in the same way be submissive to your husbands so that, if any of them do not believe the word, they may be won over without words by the behavior of their wives, when they see the purity and reverence of your lives.

Ephesians 5:22 (NIV) Wives, submit to your husbands as to the Lord.

The Bible is specific in the husband-wife relationship. As married women, we are called to submit to our husbands *as to the Lord*. Bluntly put, this means how we treat our husbands is also an act of *life worship* to God. Stop and think about this concept for a moment. We worship our Savior with how we treat our husbands. Sound strange?

I grew up thinking respect was earned. Your actions and your words determined if you were worthy of being respected. I loved the Aretha Franklin song, R-E-S-P-E-C-T. As a child, I would sing it loud and strong. Our culture reinforces this misconception. According to the Bible as Christian women, we are instructed to respect our husbands if for nothing more, than the role they have in our lives – that's a Godly perspective. The Bible does not say our husbands must earn our respect by doing what we want them to do. It clearly states we are to respect them for their God given authority in our lives.

Ephesians 5:33 (NIV) However, each one of you (men) also must love his wife as he loves himself, and the wife must respect her husband.

For me this was a difficult concept to grasp. I grew up believing respect should be earned and here, in God's Word, it is opposite. Respect is anticipated from the first day we said, "I do." It is freely given. Not earned, but given. Take some time and ask yourself – do I show my husband Godly respect?

We all make mistakes...

It was a Saturday night, and I will forever remember it as the night I realized I was disrespectful. I was determinedly growing my relationship with Christ and trying desperately to follow His Word. My husband was at a NASCAR race with friends and called me on his friend's cell phone since his phone was dead. I could tell they were having a good time. After he said goodbye, he thought his friend hung up the phone, but we were still connected. I listened intently to the conversation the men were having, and the longer I listened the faster the blood raced through my body and eventually to my hot-tempered head. After about 20 minutes, I could take no more so I hung up. I called one of the other guys on the trip and told him to tell my husband that I just overheard their conversation and he needed to call me immediately. My two sweet children were watching a movie in my bed at the time and due to my rage, overheard our entire conversation. I verbally slammed their father repeatedly in front of them. This was disrespect in full force. The reconciliation after this battle took weeks.

Respect and submission does not mean you become a spineless person. It does not mean you suffer abuse. What it does mean is that you put the other person above you in conversation and deeds.

If your spouse is forcing you to do something immoral, illegal, or harmful to others, you are not to follow him. If you are married to a man who enjoys using you or your children as punching bags you are excluded as well. Get out of those situations immediately because God never intended for his daughters to be abused. Let's be clear on this point. God appoints *you* as a *co-heir with Jesus* which is completely opposite from being a doormat or punching bag.

By surrendering yourself spiritually to your husband's authority, you are unifying your home around God's original order. I know what some of you are thinking. Trust me, I was once a strong-minded female administrator who was focused on my career and goals. I thought my first priority should be myself, then my kids and then my husband. I watched numerous television shows and read countless books on how to improve myself. I was completely absorbed in what I now call the *ME* lie. God's plan for me was opposite from the life I was living. I needed to change my perspective and I knew it. I challenge you to ask God what changes He wants to make in your life so you can facilitate spiritual order in your home. Think about refocusing your life on serving your family; with God first, husband second and children third.

The entire time I was working my way up the corporate ladder I wasn't happy. I was merely dragging myself through my daily routine. My fake smile told the world I was happy; but it was a lie. I am amazed and so incredibly thankful God brought me to a place in my life where He opened my eyes and refocused my life.

A different perspective...

Let's take a little time and think about this concept of serving in your home. In your workplace, are you the best? Do you see your boss's or co-workers' needs and assist them before being asked? Are you constantly analyzing ways to avoid conflict and resolve issues? Then, you are already a submitted servant at work. This is the exact concept our Heavenly Father wants us to implement in our homes. Anticipate what your husband's needs are. Position him first. I know, this is a difficult notion and takes countless hours of practice if a new concept. It was for me. However, this is how Jesus conducted himself while on earth, and He is our ultimate example. The truth is Jesus came here to serve and not be served. Our lives should be modeled after His. We are to serve, submit and then watch God write the story of the rest of our lives.

Matthew 20:28 (NIV) Just as the Son of Man did not come to be served but to serve and to give his life as a ransom for many.

I have witnessed the life changing power of Jesus in my home. At one time, I thought I would just suffer until my children were adults and then get a divorce. At that time, my only thoughts were of myself and what I thought would make me happy. Today, I *could not imagine* my life without my husband. While he is far from perfect, he loves Jesus and our family more than words can explain. He leads men to Christ and always prays on his knees, which I love. My husband's relationship with Jesus started to grow when I decided to align my home with the spiritual order God designed.

In the beginning of trying to change my thought process regarding my role and my husband's role in my home, I did not view it as submitting to him but submitting to God. This thought process was easier for me because when I started I was full of anger. It is easy to look at your husband at times and think he is not as smart as you are or he is not making the best decisions. We KNOW God created the heavens, the earth, and all things on the earth. Therefore, submitting to Him was much easier in my mind than submitting to my husband. My husband is only human, and will continue to do things that irritate me, so will yours. I also recognized that I was human and the negative thought patterns that plagued me did not disappear overnight.

What I learned was a new way to worship Jesus. The way I interacted with my spouse became worship because I was making a conscious effort to put him first even in situations where others might say I was crazy. Let me be super specific here on what this looks like. First, I no longer argued about every little thing. My first step was learning how to control my mouth. Remember, when I started this process my husband was not all about God. Therefore, I was living with a man, who at times, would belittle me and make fun of my faith. Sound familiar? Keep going.

I spent countless hours in my bathroom during that first year. Every time I was tempted to slam him with my mouth or belittle him (which was my habit), I would go to my bathroom, pray and ask God for specific direction on what to do. God would respond with this one phase, which became my motto, *walk in love.*

In 1 Peter wives are instructed to submit and be gentle. When I first read this, it was a foreign concept to my personality. So I decided to do some research. The Greek meaning for being gentle (*Greek: praus, meek, humble*) is a mark of strength rather than weakness. The word was frequently used in ancient literature to refer to a wild beast that had been tamed, *suggesting the characteristic is acquired rather than natural.* I loved that! Now I had hope. By overlooking my husband's irritants and trying to demonstrate God's love, our relationship became my *Life Worship* to God. There were countless times during this process I walked out of the room and reminded myself I was submitting to God. Sometimes I still do.

The change...

At first, my husband was dumbfounded. Looking back, he says he thought it was another ploy to get him to do what I wanted him to do. It was only after he realized, I was no longer playing games but serious about changing my life for Jesus that he took me seriously. What can be more rewarding as a daughter of the King, knowing you are living life His way? There is a supernatural power, which comes from submitting to God. It changes everything. I want you to stop right here and think about what you want changed in your home. Ask yourself are you willing to allow God to make those changes? Are you sick of living a life with something missing, a hollow existence, just going through the motions convinced there is nothing more?

Regardless of the problems, you have in your marriage, if you bring them before God with an open heart, He can and still does work miracles! My marriage today is a living testimony to God's mercy and grace. I urge you to start by going to God and confessing any anger or even hatred you have in your heart concerning your husband. Give your anger to the Lord; ask God for forgiveness, and God will replace the anger and hatred with peace. This act of surrendering will become a daily ritual in the beginning of your submission journey. How long will it take, you ask? It may take several months or several years, but do not give up.

I deeply understand this concept, and even today, after years of submission, the ugly disrespect monster tries to rise up in me from time to time. Why? Because the enemy will remind me of the days when my husband would make crude jokes with my kids and call me the *church lady*. I must be on guard at all times and make a conscious effort to be respectful.

What works for me is this. I keep my mouth shut, and sometimes I leave the room. I give any growing anger to God by simply saying, "God take it, here it comes again." I can smile about this now, but at one time, I could not. I could only thrash it around in my heart with fury. Please do not get discouraged – changing your heart takes time. The awesome thing is you are moving in God's direction, and He will embrace you as you run into his arms.

One thing I learned was determination was required. I found myself many times lying down and picking back up the same old issue. I learned God couldn't really free me of a struggle unless I am truly prepared to give it to Him.

God can change your heart but you must be seriously willing. He makes changes in us **as we allow ourselves to be changed**. If you are willing to give God some of your nasty but not all – your results will not be true freedom. God can only make miraculous changes in your life when you totally surrender your will to His. He doesn't play games. I know because I tried to give God some of my nasty, not all of my nasty– but it really doesn't work that way.

Take some time to think about your normal day and how often you are faced with situations you would rather fight than submit. The truth is you may start this submission journey thinking it is about your marriage and in reality, it is about your heart. You will need encouragement along the way. I recommend you keep a journal and write down every time you see a little victory in your spouse. On rough days, this will be your encouragement. I think of these moments in my life as Jesus' kisses. Here's one time Jesus kissed me totally expectedly.

When we get out of the way...

The trip to visit my parents in Kentucky took six hours from our home in Ohio. I hate to be in a car for more than four hours so the last two were always a little tortuous. To make the trip even more unbearable, my husband would always listen to ESPN radio–I hated this! Oh my word! I would put on headphones and listen to Christian music or try to sleep which was never successful.

The first time it happened I seriously almost peed my pants. Without any offensive looks or any encouraging words my husband turned the dial to a contemporary Christian radio station and pulled the car out of the driveway. I did not know what to do. You know those times when you want to jump up and down with joy – that is exactly how I felt but I dare not show it. My heart smiled and to myself I said, "Thank you God!"

Here's one more. Several years ago, I spent three hours after church one Sunday cleaning a house the new Associate Pastor was going to move into while knowing my own house was in need of a good cleaning. Ladies, you know the anxiety of having housework to do but not having time to do it. Well, that is exactly where my mind was. I had to keep reminding myself serving others is *Life Worship* and eventually my house would get cleaned. All day I kept trying to let the anxiety go.

It was about 4:00 pm when I headed home. I walked up the entry way and to my surprise my home smelled of cleaning products. You know that smell. It just makes you smile to think about it. My husband and kids had completely cleaned our home from top to bottom. I was totally amazed, and my eyes quickly filled with tears. This my friends was a God kiss given to me from my Heavenly Father to say "Stay encouraged! I see your heart and you are moving in my direction."

God knows what needs to change in your heart and in your home. As God changes you, He will also make changes in your husband and children that will stun and amaze you. For every God kiss you receive, give God all the glory and praise He deserves. It is a step toward your heaven on earth.

Matthew 7:7-8 (NIV) Jesus said, "Ask and it will be given to you; seek and you will find; knock and the door will be opened to you. For everyone who asks receives; he who seeks finds; and to him who knocks, the door will be opened."

Questions for thought...

    1) Do you blow your husband up verbally? Why?

    2) Do you feel the need to win every argument?

    3) What is one thing your husband could do that would light up your heart? Start praying about this.

Action steps...

The first step you need to take is learning to control your mouth. I know this is difficult; it was a tough lesson for me but it truly is life changing. Find a spot in your home where you can be alone with God and go there every time you find yourself ready to bring out the big verbal guns and blow your husband away. This will take time. Ask Jesus to give you self-control. He will and you will be surprised at what will happen next.

Chapter 5

Faith

The warm sun on my face, the cool grass beneath my legs and the cotton ball like clouds cascading across the sky. I remember lying in the grass as a child and staring at the sky and wondering what was on the other side. I knew even then God was real and up there. I wasn't sure why He was watching me, but I knew He was. One of the things I appreciate about having a Preacher for a Father is that I never doubted God was real and up there.

For others faith is an understanding that does not come so easily. I think one of the best ways to begin to understand the word faith is to go to the book of Romans and read the 4th chapter. It says in part …

*Romans: 4:3 (NIV) "Abraham **believed** God, and it was credited to him as righteousness… It was not through law that Abraham and his offspring received the promise that he would be heir of the world, but through the righteousness that comes by faith.*

Continue in this chapter and you'll realize Abraham was about one hundred years old when this part of his story took place. He was not in the most fertile age group, but **believed** what God said would happen and it did – he became a father at the ripe old age of one hundred years. This faith concept may be a little harder for some of you. We are called as Christians to live by faith. Faith is defined according to Webster's Online Dictionary as **complete trust**. Faith is knowing God is in control, and He loves us no matter where we are in life. It means if you are short on cash and you have bills to be paid, you pray, **believe** and God will make a way for payment. It doesn't mean God will give you the winning lottery numbers. It means He will make a way. This way may come in the form of a better job, a friend giving you a loan, the debt payment beginning extended, but a way will come.

Every day, you pray, **believe** and leave the rest to God. You may be saying, what exactly am I supposed to **believe**? You are called to **believe** God will supply **everything** you need to live. Don't take this the wrong way, I'm not saying you should quit your job and just start expecting money to fall from the sky. I'm saying according to God's Word, He promises to supply all of our needs if we **believe.**

Another Jesus kiss...

The first time I saw his face, I was in love. For the past year my motherly instincts had been churning, and I could no longer contain myself–I wanted a puppy. I was in my late thirties, and the desire just would not go away. I wanted something that needed me. My family already had two cats (which I did not care for), and all I could think of was a sweet little puppy with puppy breath that I could call my own. Now that I was living submitted to God, my new way of thinking was to ask my husband's permission. You see, both of the cats just kind of showed up at my house without my husband's prior knowledge. I wanted to do this right. I did and guess what? He was completely against it. He did not want the third animal in our home and would not even talk about it.

I decided to start praying about it. I asked God according to His Will to either change my husband's heart or mine. I was dedicated to this prayer every day. After about six months I felt the Holy Spirit encouraging me to discuss the topic with my husband again. This time it was approaching my 40th birthday. I remember uncertainty of the outcome swirling in my stomach as I walked into the living room where my husband was watching the local news. I wisely waited until it was over and said. "Honey, can I talk to you for a minute." He smiled and said "Sure, what's up?" I asked once again if he would consider me getting a puppy this time for my birthday. I knew in my heart if he said "no" again that was it, and I would have no choice but to drop it. My heart was pounding. Silence filled the room. Next, to my total and complete surprise he asked me why I wanted a puppy. I told him I had been praying about it for the past six months, and I knew it was the right time for us to increase our family in this way.

Again he was silent. I knew from my days as a salesperson – once you make the pitch you remain silent until the potential buyer speaks. He looked me in the eye and said, "Now, how can I argue with that?" I almost seriously passed out. This was another Jesus kiss! I jumped up ran over, gave him a big hug and kiss, and told him how much I loved him.

Within the next month I brought home our little Shorky (Shih Tzu and Yorky mix) named Dusty. I think at times my husband loves this dog more than I do. He has become a loving part of our family, and we cannot imagine life without him. This ladies is the power of faith in prayer.

James 1:6-8 (NIV) But when he asks, he must believe and not doubt, because he who doubts is like a wave of the sea, blown and tossed by the wind. That man should not think he will receive anything from the Lord.

This scripture clearly says not to doubt – specific to our prayer life. When we ask God for things we are not to doubt but come with the understanding that we are talking to our Creator and not a genie. He provides what aligns with His will in His time, not always ours. What happens in your heart when you pray for a while, wait and nothing? Do you begin to doubt? Is doubt a sin?

Let's dig in here and focus for a minute on doubt. We first see doubt in the Bible in the book of Genesis chapter three when satan is tempting Eve. God had given her a direct command regarding *one* tree and the apples growing there. Did He not? Yes He did. Oh Ladies, how many times in our lives are we tempted by the *one thing*? The one thing that we know is not good for us? How many times do we give into fleshy desires that we know are not good for us? Satan was, and is today, clever at using doubt against a Jesus follower. Let's look at his words which grew a seed of doubt in Eve's mind.

Genesis 3:1-4 (NIV) Now the serpent was more crafty than any of the wild animals the LORD God had made. He said to the woman, "Did God really say, 'You must not eat from any tree in the garden'?"[2] The woman said to the serpent, "We may eat fruit from the trees in the garden, ³ but God did say, 'You must not eat fruit from the tree that is in the middle of the garden, and you must not touch it, or you will die.'"⁴ "You will not certainly die," the serpent said to the woman. ⁵ "For God knows that when you eat from it your eyes will be opened, and you will be like God, knowing good and evil."

It was actions Eve chose that were sinful. The fact Eve doubted God was not a sin it was the action that the doubt led her to. Let's look at this scenario. What if after the conversation with satan, Eve waited until the evening, and simply asked God about the serpent's banter. In this scenario she would have dealt with her doubt in a positive way. If only she had not acted upon her doubt there could have been a completely different outcome and our men would be having babies. (Yes you should be laughing). Doubting in and of itself is not a sin. However, if you allow doubt to lead you away from God then yes it is not good. I wonder how many of you have asked God for something, and it has not been granted. Why didn't my Heavenly Father heal my earthly father when I asked or why didn't Jesus heal my marriage when I asked? Why did God allow cancer to take my friend? I don't have all the answers, but the Creator does. He does everything for a reason in His time. Again, this is part of our faith challenge. It could be He is growing you spiritually or it is just not the right time for your requests. This is when faith gets hard. Part of your spiritual journey is believing and accepting that He knows what is best even when it is not what you requested. This is challenging at times to understand. I recognize this because I have walked through some tough situations too. Without my faith in God I would just give up, go to bed and quit life. But the Word of God encourages me.

John 20:29 (NIV) Then Jesus told him, "Because you have seen me, you have believed; blessed are those who have not seen and yet have believed."

Tears streamed down my face as it was time to say goodbye. I didn't want to let her go but I didn't have a choice. I understand what it feels like when the answer to your prayer is "no." I had a sweet friend with cancer, and I prayed for a long time she would be healed. However, God decided her healing would take place in heaven. During her cancer journey I had the privilege to walk it out with her and know she was going to see Jesus. I would have loved to have kept her here longer but that too was not God's plan. I think one of the most important parts of faith is **believing** when it is not easy. **Believing** when your heart feels like it is getting ripped out of your chest. **Believing** when those around you, due to your circumstances think you are nuts. That's faith, and, that's what I'm talking about.

Faith is hard for many people who feel they need to see something in order to believe it. Don't let satan get a grip on your mind and persuade you to follow his lies and deceit, remember Eve. If you will slow down, look around, and open your eyes to the Creator's handiwork in every flower, every sunset; you will see the Almighty.

Hebrews 11:1 (NIV) ...Now faith is being sure of what we hope for and certain of what we do not see.

Continue and read Hebrews the eleventh chapter and you will find many examples of faith. Noah's faith saved his family. Abraham's faith gave him a son and many nations. Moses' faith set God's people free, and on and on. Take a serious look at what types of tasks these people were given. How do those compare with your life? Jesus may not be asking you to build an ark or set a group of people free but following Him is just as important. He is asking you to believe. When I stop and think about the examples of faith in the Bible, I am quick to feel extremely humbled. If God is asking me to serve my family and my church, by faith, I need to do what I am called and not worry. It seems so incredibly small in comparison to the tasks given to Moses and Noah. I get chills just thinking about what was running through Noah's mind working night and day to get ready for the flood while everyone thought he was crazy.

Whining is just annoying...
I was sitting in church one Sunday and the lady in front of me was having a difficult time with her son. He would not sit still and yet cried profusely when she tried to leave him in the pre-school room. I felt bad for her. I felt bad for him. Then it started. I don't know why

but this little adorable boy started whining. I mean really loud during the Pastor's message. He didn't want to sit still. He didn't want to be silenced. He didn't want to do anything but tell everyone around him that he was not happy. His mother took all she could stand and then yanked him up and left the room. I sat there thinking about how no matter what she did, she was unable in that moment to make her child stop whining. I thought about how our Heavenly Father must see us just like that little boy from time to time. We don't receive what we ask for, so eventually we moan about it.

This is another important aspect of our faith walk – don't whine. Okay, I know sometimes, especially every twenty-seven days or so we as women get cranky and may have a tendency to moan a little. However, some believe to share their hardship of being a Christian is an acceptable practice. I must disagree. The Bible is extremely clear this "poor me" attitude is not the righteousness expected. This is not God-like behavior. We are called to have faith which should release us from the sin of grumbling.

Philippians 2: 14-16 (NIV) Do everything without complaining or arguing, so that you may become blameless and pure, children of God, without fault in a crooked and depraved generation, in which you shine like stars in the universe.

The reference section in the NIV versions adds: Complaining – being discontented with God's will is an expression of unbelief that prevents one from doing what pleases God. You see, ladies, when we complain we are telling the Lord we are not happy with what His plan is for us. We are literally sucking all of the potential good out of the situation. This does not demonstrate our faith. This definitely does not please Jesus to hear. Remember the story of Jonah and the whale? God asked him to go to one place, Nineveh and preach against the wickedness of the people. But Jonah didn't want to listen. He disobeyed and ended up in the belly of a whale. He cried out in prayer for the Lord to save him.

Jonah 2:2 (NIV) "In my distress I called to the Lord and he answered me. From the depths of the grave I called for help, and you listened to my cry. You hurled me into the deep into the very heart of the seas and the currents swirled about me; all your waves and breakers swept over me."

I don't know about you, but I really would like to avoid hardship brought about due to my direct disobedience, lack of faith and grumbling to God. Jonah received a second chance. Luckily God grants us another chance each day to get it right and exercise our faith. If you are in a grumbling mood right now I want you to stop and just say "Jesus loves me, Jesus loves ME!" That is the truth and should put a smile back on that grumpy face. What does our faith look like? We know no matter what tomorrow may hold the Creator of the universe loves us beyond our imagination and He will never leave us. This confidence, this hope, this truth will move us forward.

Questions for thought...

1) Do you believe that God is who He says He is in the Bible?

2) Do you believe that God can do all things that the Bible says He can do?

3) Are you living your life fully by trusting God today?

Action steps...

If you are struggling to wrap your brain around who God is, then spend some time in the book of Matthew and read about the life of Jesus. This book is full of the personality of our Lord. Allow the truth of God's Word to penetrate your heart. Pray for strength and wisdom. Think of your Bible reading as a way to learn more about a new best friend rather than a chore. I'm praying for you now that God begins to grow an unquenchable thirst in your heart for His Word.

Chapter 6
Patience

One morning after eight months of practicing submission in my home, I awoke-brain swirling. When was my husband going to move closer to God? Was his transformation EVER going to happen? The entire day I tried to push it out of my mind but just like a yo-yo it kept returning. By the end of day I found myself frustrated and angry. I was in my bedroom, making the bed, and a book peering out from the dust ruffle caught my eye. I leaned down, picked it up and to my surprise it was an old journal which I had kept my "Jesus kisses" in. I opened it up and read an entry from six months ago. "So if nothing more happens, I will die a happy woman. For God continues to answer my prayers. Today for the first time we had a family Bible study and we all prayed together. Three years ago this would have NEVER happened. Then, we prayed together as a family, and each person talked about their day. My husband actually got down on his knees to pray. I cried like a baby. Jesus overwhelms me with His blessings and how He continues to change my man."

Somehow, I had forgotten how far we had traveled. Our marriage will never be perfect but change was happening and I knew more than anything else, I needed to be patient, thankful and full of faith.

Colossians 1:10-11(NIV) "And we pray this in order that you may live a life worthy of the Lord and may please him in every way: bearing fruit in every good work, growing in the knowledge of God, being strengthened with all power according to his glorious might so that you may have great endurance and patience, and joyfully giving thanks to the Father..

Colossians 3:12 (NIV) "Therefore, as God's chosen people, holy and dearly loved, clothe yourselves with compassion, kindness and patience."

Unlimited patience...

What does patience look like in our daily lives? For some it may be quite different than others. My favorite example of patience is remembering the two weeks before Christmas when I was a child. I was totally euphoric! I would walk around the house singing, dancing and saying "Merry Christmas," to everyone all the time. Just the thought of what was coming filled my heart with pure joy. I knew it was coming, and I was exultant; no I actually savored the countdown.

Can you imagine the freedom we would experience if when waiting on our Heavenly Father to answer a prayer request, we responded like children at Christmas? I wasn't always sure of what my present was going to be, but I knew it would be awesome. Just like in our prayer requests, we don't always receive what we ask for. Sometimes it is not in the time frame we would like; however, it is always perfect for us because it is God's plan.

1 Timothy 1:15-16 (NIV) Here is a trustworthy saying that deserves full acceptance: Christ Jesus came into the world to save sinners – of whom I am the worst. But for that very reason I was shown mercy so that in me, the worst of sinners, Christ Jesus might display his unlimited patience as an example for those who would believe on him and receive eternal life.

Did you notice the words "unlimited patience" in the previous scripture? What does that look like? Can you wrap your brain around it? I think of when my daughter was learning to walk. She loved to roll all over the floor but walking she was not so sure about. Her father and I would encourage her, hold our hands out and she would just smile, sit back down and play. We thought *wow is this kid ever going to walk*? I picture Jesus looking at us exactly the same. He is encouraging us to move closer to Him. His hands are outstretched, and how many times do we sit rather than walk?

We are called to be "Christ-like," exhibiting the traits that Christ did while He was on this earth. I don't know about you, but I need specific examples in order to truly understand behavior, what it could look like in my life, and what is expected of me. Jesus gave us His life as this example recorded in the Bible. We must take His example, digest it and allow the Holy Spirit to be our decision maker. We must allow the Holy Spirit to drive us each day – just like our bodies are cars in a NASCAR race and the Holy Spirit is in the driver's seat. (My husband is a fan and will love the fact I worked that in here.) The lesson can be easy to miss but sometimes by not giving us what we are praying for God is doing us a favor.

Let God be God...

I wrote the numbers down one more time and added them praying they were actually less than what I just totaled a minute ago. To my dismay the numbers were exactly the same. The problem was, the number I was staring at was the total of our monthly family budget. Unfortunately, our total family income was going to be lower than that once I was no longer employed. I closed my eyes and prayed for God to give me clear direction. God was calling me into full time ministry. It was something my heart longed for but my bank account was not cooperating.

So what did I do? Did I wait patiently on the Lord? Not really. I sent a message to my current employer stating that if they wanted me to continue employment, I would be willing to do so. The only reason I was willing to stay was to pay our bills. However, God had other plans. To my surprise the company said, "No thank you," and I realized my mistake. I was not waiting on the Lord. I was not being patient. I was trying to control my destiny which is not my job. I repented and asked God for His Will and not my will be done. I was resigned to wait with joy in my heart as His plans are always better than mine.

Guess what? At exactly the perfect moment, the Almighty encouraged two people to bless us with a financial gift toward our new life adventure. I cried. I praised Him. Even though I experienced some pain in the process, the outcome was so much better than anything

I could have asked for. That is how our Heavenly Father works. We just have to give Him a chance to be God in our lives.

Hebrews 6:12 (NIV) "We do not want you to become lazy, but to imitate those who through faith and patience inherit what has been promised."

I love the scripture above because it combines faith with patience. When I think about Biblical examples of faith, of course, Abraham comes to mind.

Hebrews 6:14 (NIV) "I will surely bless you and give you many descendants."

In case you are unaware of Abraham and Sarah's story, they desperately wanted a child but found themselves at an old age and childless. God not only gave them a son but also made them the parents of all nations. What I love most about this story is their humanity. It is not a fairytale. They made some vast mistakes during the journey, one of which was Sarah encouraging her husband to sleep with their maid. They experienced the consequences of their mistakes, but they also experienced the faithfulness of God's promise to Abraham. He trusted and believed, and his son Isaac went on to be the beginning of "many decedents."

For most of us we want our prayers answered now. These may be perfectly positive prayers such as healings, restorations and salvation. However, Jesus is not a genie. He has a plan and purpose for your life and His time is usually different than ours.

Father God cannot change the circumstances in your life until your focus is all about loving and obeying Him. Not *when will my dreams come true?* He wants desperately to bless you and to show you just how much He loves you. But, He can't do that if you are constantly checking the clock. I advise you to put the clock away. Tell God you understand it is His time and not yours. Ask Him to give you peace so you are not tempted to even think about how long you have been praying over the same thing.

How many of you want Jesus to change your spouse? How many of you look at other Christian men and think *if only* my husband was more like that. Do I hear an Amen? Well, I know from experience; beating your husband over the head with your Bible will only leave a bruise and one exhausted woman. If you want your man to become the Christian home leader, the way God designed it, it all starts with you. Yes, that's what I said YOU. You must first submit to God. This means making the decision you want a Jesus relationship more than anything and taking action to get to know Him. It also means you are willing to submit to your husband. You see, once you get yourself out of the way, God can finally start working on him...

Life Change...

It was a really awesome study. The Bible was coming alive for me, and I finally was beginning to understand the steps I needed to take to move closer to Jesus. Additionally, I was actually starting to make friends! As the Bible study came to a close, I stood around and talked with a couple of my newfound girlfriends. Then I jumped in my car a little excited to go home and share with my husband a couple of insights. Maybe he would listen. When I walked in the door, it was oddly quiet. As I turned to go up the stairs my husband was standing at the top with an angry look on his face. You see, in Bible study I put my phone on silent and forgot to turn the ringer back on. My hubby had been trying to contact me because he wanted me to pick up a pizza on my way home. My smile quickly disappeared as he began yelling over the lack of communication and his starving stomach. My mind raced; my neck splotched. I wanted to scream! However I didn't, rather with every ounce of constraint I could muster up, I said, "I'm sorry, next time I'll check my phone." I headed straight to my bathroom because I needed to *talk* to God. With tears already rolling down my face I said deafeningly, "God this is your man and your problem and you deal with him!" and I said nothing further.

Was I upset? Sure I was. Did I cry? Yes I did. I was determined to handle the situation as godly as I possibly could. Since I submitted the situation to the Almighty, instead of trying to resolve it myself, the outcome was actually better than I could have imagined.

For the next two days my husband apologized repeatedly. He not only apologized to me but our children as well. He confessed to us all that he was totally out of line and asked for our forgiveness. This was amazing! Normally, he would have said "I'm sorry" one time. I would not have actually accepted it, and turmoil would have continued for several days. However, his eyes were full of regret, and his apology was heartfelt. He was ashamed of his behavior. God had convicted his soul (all without my interference imagine that) and propelled remorse that went racing through his veins. This is a **gigantic** lesson for us ladies, and one that can change your marriage. God is the master at turning the heart of your man; your bitter words and heated attitudes are ineffective.

*1 Peter 3:7 Husbands, in the same way be considerate as you live with your wives, and treat them with respect as the weaker partner and as heirs with you of the gracious gift of life, **so that nothing will hinder your prayers**.*

According to the NIV study notes *"hinder your prayers"* means the spiritual fellowship with God and with one another, may be hindered by disregarding God's instruction concerning husband-wife relationships. The Almighty holds your husband accountable for his actions. God can change your man, but a life change takes time and time is His.

This *life change* is real. It can happen. I am living proof. I was once so bound up in **my** time, I couldn't see the forest for the trees. God has shown me repeatedly once I surrendered my clock to Him, I found peace. Yes, actual peace in the middle of what should be turbulent times. Don't misunderstand there are still things I would like to change in my home. However, today I can say to God, "in Your time, not mine, and thank you for what is coming."

Patience is not always easy but it is something **you can choose to exercise**. If it doesn't come naturally to you, re-program your mind. When you begin to feel impatient, just stop and remember God will bless you if you wait on His timing. Write down the scripture verses in this chapter that spoke to you on an index card and keep it in your purse. When you are faced with the challenge to exercise patience, pull it out and read it out loud. It is an awesome way to gain instant peace and meditate on the Word.

If you are still struggling with the issue of patience, I recommend that you spend some time thinking about how patient our Heavenly Father is with you each day. There is nothing better to bring us back to reality than to think about our own mistakes and sins and how God continues to have patience with us. It helps to put this topic in perspective when you look at it from God's point of view.

One of the greatest examples of God's *"unlimited patience"* was when the Israelites' were in the desert. Here we have His chosen people wandering around for forty years on a journey which should have taken less than two weeks because of their lack of faith and obedience. Yet, our Heavenly Father exercised patience with them and continued to love them and wait until they were truly ready to see the Promised Land. Talk about patience!

Have you wandered around in your own desert for a number of years? Is God waiting for you so He can take you into the land of milk and honey – the Promised Land in your very home? The sad thing is, so many times in our lives we are not even aware we are in a wasteland. The desert surroundings have become so familiar it appears normal to us. If you think you are in a desert, pray the prayer below. Even if you've been in your wilderness for forty years – **it's not too late**. As long as you have breath in your body, it is not too late to give God the keys to your heart.

Father God, I come before you now recognizing that I have spent too much time in this desert. I know you have better things for me so I surrender to you now my will, I repent of my disobedience and ask you to forgive me of my sin. Father please show me what to do next and how to move forward into my Promised Land. I love you Jesus, and I will follow you wherever you want me to go. Strengthen me, change me, and grow me into what I need to be for you. Thank you for the journey ahead and what is coming. In Jesus name I pray. Amen.

Questions for thought...

1) Is there something you have been waiting for in prayer?

2) Are you truly allowing God to be God in your home or are you still trying to be the *controller*?

3) Are you ready to give God the authority to be fully God in your home?

Action steps...

I understand at times it is difficult to wait on God. We have all been there at one time or another. Yet, it is during this time of waiting that we grow spiritually as we release our control and accept His. If you have never verbally given God full authority in our home, that is a great place to start. Remember the visual of children waiting on Christmas and allow that thought to push you into a positive waiting position.

Chapter 7

*W*hat is a stronghold you ask? Think of the name for its definition–something strong holding you back from living the life of freedom God plans for you. Anything standing in the way of you getting closer to God is a stronghold. Are you aware off the top of your head of any strongholds which are keeping you from enjoying the life God has intended for you? Trust me–we all have them whether or not we are aware of them. When I first asked myself that question, I couldn't come up with an answer right away. I didn't think I had any really. I never stopped and gave it much thought until I was challenged to ask God what my strongholds were. Believe me if you are ready to get serious and dig into getting closer to God, He will bring your strongholds to the surface.

Sometimes strongholds enjoy hanging out in the back of our minds undetected from our daily routine. The first thing you must be aware of is–a stronghold is not something you can deal with by yourself. The desire to overcome a stronghold is the first step. You will need the supernatural power of the Holy Spirit to shatter it.

2 Corinthians 10:3-5 "For though we live in the world, we do not wage war as the world does. The weapons we fight with are not the weapons of the world. On the contrary, they have divine power to demolish strongholds. We demolish arguments and every pretension that sets itself up against the knowledge of God, as we take captive every thought to make it obedient to Christ."

This scripture really hits the nail on the head regarding our mind as a battlefield. We are told to take captive **every** thought we have and make it obedient to God. I don't know about you, but I used to have hundreds, no thousands of thoughts each day that were not pleasing to God. Little things, like when I was driving, and I had road rage. I would call the other drivers names, like "You need glasses grandma!" or "Where did you learn to drive!" and on and on. Let's just say when I was driving, my mind was usually racing with the twenty things on my *to-do list*, and the reason all of the other cars were making me late!

However, now my attitude is different. I actually think about the person driving. Maybe the person in front of me is also having a bad day. Maybe they just received bad health news or someone they loved just died. Taking a few moments to consider others rather than ourselves will totally change our perspective, it has mine.

Taking control of your mind is the first major step in being able to break and remain free of any strongholds in your life. Thoughts eventually become words, actions or both, so completely recognizing your mind is the greatest battleground is the first step to breaking a stronghold. Let's face it; satan greatly enjoys tangling up our minds with negative, depressive and angry thoughts. He is real, and the battle is real. We must see these things for what they are; ploys to distract us from God and His will for us. You cannot enjoy God's peace if your brain is full of nasty thoughts.

Don't kid yourself by thinking whatever stronghold you have you can deal with alone. Christians will never truly experience the joy and peace God designed for us without allowing the Holy Spirit to free us from our strongholds. We may not be aware of it, but strongholds affect our daily thinking and our behavior.

Self-preservation has a price…

The day I saw the envelope with the laminated orange card inside my heart started to pound out of my chest. It was from the Radio Broadcasters Association. In my hands at the age of sixteen, I held a license to be a Disc Jockey. It sounded so glamorous! My Sister worked at our local radio station and would take me to work with her on weekends. I loved it.

It was Christmas Eve, and my Sister was scheduled to close the station that night. I was glad to go with her. Christmas music filled the air and my mind continued to bounce to what was waiting at home – presents, food, and family all good things. I watched the clock and before I knew it, we were walking to her car singing the last song that played tonight, *We Wish You A Merry Christmas* out loud for all to hear. Pulling into our driveway I could hardly contain myself. Yes, I was sixteen but Christmas was my **favorite** holiday (and still is).

I'll never forget walking in the door, and my eyes immediately focused on the Christmas tree. Only five presents remained. Earlier that day the Christmas tree skirt was nowhere to be found under the massive pile of presents. All of the other carefully wrapped gifts that were there only hours ago had disappeared. There was a party going on, and everyone was having a wonderful time. My head started to spin as I looked at all of the happy faces trying to find my mother. What in the world happened? Why did they open everyone's presents without me? I decided to give up my search as my eyes swelled with tears. I raced to my room, threw myself on my bed and began crying hysterically.

Eventually my mother came in to check on me and see why I was not joining the party. I can't remember exactly what I said, but I do remember throwing a near-by orange at her as she closed the door to leave. That was the day I decided I needed to protect myself. I couldn't allow people to hurt my heart so deeply. Therefore, the first layer of insulation was quickly wrapped around my heart. Throughout my teenage years I continued to put security measures in place for my own protection. Little by little, I constructed a dense rubber wall around my heart in order to survive.

In my late teens I experienced one of the most horrific moments all young ladies pray will never happen. I decided to surprise my boyfriend for his birthday. His car was in the driveway so I knew he was home. With balloons in hand I slowly opened the front door, but he was nowhere to be found. I heard some noise coming from the bedroom so I quietly tip toed toward his bedroom and opened the half closed door. Guess what? There he was in bed with another girl. I didn't know what to do. I let go of the balloons and ran. Needless to say, I never spoke to him again. I tried to repair my broken heart by vowing never to let myself care so deeply for someone. The wall around my heart thickened.

I have been employed somewhere since I was sixteen. My parents always stressed that hard work was a sign of good character. I found self-worth in employment and doing a job well. On one of my first jobs I found myself one day called into the boss's office. The night before, a supervisor pinned me up against a wall and said, "What would you do if I kissed you right now?" I started laughing. I was so young. It did nothing for his ego. The next day he reported me for being immature in the workplace. I was seventeen. I did keep my job and my mouth shut. Another layer of protection was placed around my heart. Heartbreak after heartbreak, I enclosed my heart in an impenetrable rubber ball. I could feel a little but not enough to allow anyone to do major damage.

I married at the young age of twenty to one of the most loving men I have ever known. I had been hurt repeatedly so my number one requirement for marriage was someone who would love me unconditionally forever. Of course marrying so young, we did experience many painful life lessons together. Life lesson after life lesson the rubber around my heart became thicker and thicker until it wasn't even a conscious effort anymore; it just happened. I loved my husband but in some odd way I was constantly holding him at arm's length so not to get hurt. I had a few acquaintances, but again, they really did not experience the real me because I didn't want to get hurt. I used to tell everyone I didn't need friends because they were too much work. With the birth of our two children, I experienced a deeper love than I had ever known. Yet, on an unconscious level even my children had not fully penetrated my protective heart.

Fast forward to my thirties. I was in a season of spiritual growth, and one of my teachers had suggested that I ask God to reveal any strongholds in my life. I thought okay but I don't think I really have any. I was so naive.

The big reveal...

It was a warm summer morning and we were vacationing in Myrtle Beach. I got up early and decided to have my morning Bible study and prayer time with a cup of coffee on the balcony. The question, "What is one of my biggest strongholds?" stirred in my mind. I was desperately questioning God to reveal any strongholds in my life which were keeping me away from Him and finally – the answer. He said clearly, "Fear." I thought what? What am I afraid of? I have you. Next He said, "Fear of loving others as I love you." Talk about totally blowing me out of the water! I was honestly not aware of this because protection had become part of my normal. He exposed me, and I could not deny it. I spent the next several days thinking about my past. I decided to write down all of the situations and/or people who hurt me and pray forgiveness through each one. I knew the time had come to unleash my heart and experience love in a way I had not since a child.

The process was not easy. It took me a couple of weeks to write it all down. Next, it took over two hours to pray through my list and one long, heart wrenching cry. When I was finished praying through my list I looked at it one last time, ripped it up and set it on fire. As the paper quickly turned to ash I knew this was a brand new road on my spiritual path. I felt lighter.

For years I carried around a fractured protected heart and was somewhat unaware of this. Not allowing myself to love deeply affected the way I treated my husband, children, family and friends. I would love them, but in a safe way. In one way, I would never get too close or really give one hundred percent of my love to anyone. It sounds sad, but it was true. I bet there are many of you out there walking around with fractured hearts.

You see, we cannot live a true life for God with a fractured heart. The rubber wall I put around my heart was also keeping me from experiencing God's true love for me. Our Heavenly Father wants more than anything for us to experience His love. His amazing, unimaginable, move mountains for us – kind of love. What I realized was that I was the one missing out on the beauty which lives in God's love. Now, it brings me to tears to think of the wasted years that I walked around with a fractured heart. Learn from my experiences and don't waste one more day allowing a fractured heart stronghold to keep you from God.

If you think your life is without strongholds, you're kidding yourself. If you are ready to let go of what is weighing you down, ask God to reveal your strongholds. Be ready; you may be surprised by what you find out about yourself. I'll never forget the day that

I finally allowed God to mend my heart. It was like a huge boulder was completely lifted from my shoulders. I felt lighter than I had in years. I looked at my family and the world around me differently. I praise God for His mercy and love and how He walked me through the repair process. You too can unlock the secret of whatever may be holding you back from a life of joy and peace with God. He **will** free you. Freedom is what the Bible promises us. Don't waste years of your life by not allowing God to heal you.

John 8:36 (NIV) Jesus said, "So if the Son sets you free, you will be free indeed."

I love this scripture because it promises us as God's children freedom from *whatever* is holding us back. The other thing ladies is that once you lay down your stronghold at the feet of Jesus, don't pick it back up. This is something I hear from women all the time. They let go of a stronghold just to pick it back up in a moment of weakness. My best advice is that you have to learn how to allow God to really be your strength. God doesn't give us strength, **He is our strength.** How do you grow your muscles? Do you just think about lifting weights? Or, do you lift weights and focus on increasing your upper body strength? It's really the same principle. If you want to strengthen your spirit you exercise it. Study your Bible. Don't just read it and think well, I can check that off my list for today. Study it. Look at other translations, read all the study notes and pray for understanding. If you make a mindful decision to grow your spirit with the Word and prayer, Jesus will meet you there. He always does.

James 4:8 (NIV) Come near to God and He will come near to you.

At one point in my life I was always after the latest *self-help* book or process or way to improve myself. Sometimes I did see small progress. It was always short lived. When I failed, I blamed myself and would drown my sorrows in food to make me feel better. Then, I came to the understanding that I was totally and completely unable to heal anything inside of me without the amazing power of the Holy Spirit of God. God has healed me from so much, and He wants to do the same for you. You just have to let Him. I know it sounds easy and some days it is. There is never any real change without effort. God will meet you where you are today. As I write this, I am praying for you. I pray whatever is separating you from our Heavenly Father, that in the name of Jesus you realize it, and walk the path of recovery with the ultimate physician, Jesus.

Questions for thought...

    1) What is holding you back from moving closer to Jesus?

    2) Do you believe that Jesus can free you from this stronghold?

    3) Are you ready to finally lay it down?

Action steps...

    Laying down a stronghold begins by recognizing it, preparing to give it to Jesus forever and finally releasing it in prayer. A stronghold only has power over you if you are allowing it. Once it is given to the Father, it no longer has any control over your life. The victory is already won so lay your stronghold at the feet of Jesus and move into your freedom.

Chapter 8

Love

Romans 8:38 (NIV) I am convinced that neither death nor life, neither angels nor demons, neither the present nor the future, nor any powers, neither height nor depth, nor anything else in all creation, will be able to separate us from the love of God that is in Christ Jesus our Lord.

*F*rom someone who was *love challenged* to someone who *loves like crazy* this verse just makes my heart leap. To know, I mean **really know**, nothing can separate us from the love of God amazes me! Love is important stuff, and the greatest command.

1 Corinthians 13:13 (NIV) And now these three remain: faith, hope and love. But the greatest of these is love.

Walk in love...

Have you ever found it hard to love? You know I have. I'm sure all of us have suffered hurt at some point in our lives. Our normal human reaction is to close down, protect ourselves and not allow our heart to feel hurt again. But be careful. It is one thing to recognize a potentially hurtful situation and still remain in God's love. It is another to place a dense rubber ball around your heart. Not being able to fully experience or show God's love is a stronghold for many people.

As God's people we are called to love the unlovely. We are called to freely give the love of our Heavenly Father to others. Now, you may be saying to yourself, "Some people don't deserve it!" I understand. I have felt that way myself from time to time. It doesn't matter how we *feel* about a particular situation or person, what matters is that we are obedient to God's Word **with each decision we make.** Remember we need to take each thought captive and make it obedient to God's Word.

1 John 15-16(NIV) Do not love the world or anything in the world. If anyone loves the world the love of the Father is not in him. For everything in the world-the cravings of sinful man, the lust of his eyes and the boasting of what he has and does- comes not from the Father, but from the world.

The vast majority of the time we cannot trust our *feelings.* Remember, human feelings are most often controlled by human external conditions – they are fleshy, worldly and not of God; which is why we must turn to Jesus for His direction in the Word each step of the way.

2 John 6 (NIV) And this is love: that we walk in obedience to His commands. As you have heard from the beginning, His command is that you walk in love.

As we walk down the path of our spiritual journey, our love for our Heavenly Father grows. Slowly, living our life God's way becomes our second nature. The last part of the scripture above was one that stays with me night and day. It is the center of our Jesus relationship. *Walk in Love.*

Have you ever had a bad habit you were able to defeat? Examples like nail biting or smoking? You had to stop and think each time you were faced with continuing in that habit or stopping. You had to make a cognizant effort to stop. It took time but eventually with the power of the Holy Spirit living inside of you, you did it. For some of us, sharing Jesus' love is like picking up a new habit. You have to stop and think about it. Make a conscious effort to do it and keep doing it. Eventually sharing God's love will become part of your daily routine. It just takes time and effort.

1 Peter 4:8 (NIV) Above all, love each other deeply, because love covers over a multitude of sins."

For me, once I removed the rubber ball from around my heart, I began to see people in a different light. I was the one who didn't want friends. Now, I was beginning to see the reason for me to seek friends was to share Jesus with them. God always has perfect timing. He gave me the opportunity to share with a young lady who I first met at my church. When I saw her later in the week at the softball field I knew this was a God thing. This young lady was not married, pregnant, and somewhat homeless. When I tried to talk to her about God, she would ask me, "So how do you know God is even real?" Rubber hearted Shari would have run in the opposite direction but God was calling me to help this girl find Him.

Over the next year, I invested myself in this young girl. I tried to show her love to the best of my ability. There were so many times I knew she thought I was crazy but I persisted. At the birth of her daughter I visited, and as I was leaving I said "I love you!" She looked at me like I had three heads. However, when she looked at that beautiful baby girl in her arms a love like she had never known encompassed her heart. I could see the door opening.

I shared with her God loves us the way she loved her baby; this was something she could now understand. It was through this child Jesus was able to reach her heart. Once she experienced motherly love then she could start to imagine how much God loved her. It was so awesome to watch this transformation in her life. She now supports herself and her child and seeks God with all of her heart. Her life has totally taken on a new direction and purpose. I give God all the glory and am amazed I was part of the story. I'll forever love this girl for she was the first person God used to show me what can happen when we love like Jesus.

We all just want to be loved...

Have you ever had a pet? I mentioned my dog Dusty earlier. Pets often give love so freely and unconditionally–especially puppies. The best is that welcome. You know what I mean every time you walk through the door they are thrilled to see you. I know my little guy barks, shakes all over and reaches his paw toward me. He is delighted when I am in the room. Pets just want to be loved. We do too, if we are honest. It is a wonderful feeling when we are the recipient of love. (I know we just talked about feelings being over-rated but stick with me here for a minute) Receiving love makes us feel as though we belong to someone or something. Love definitely provokes an emotional reaction. Can you fathom how our Heavenly Father responds when we are moved to tears by the love we have for Him? I mean, come on, this is His greatest command and seeing His children live it out must give Him great joy! It blows my mind to think the Creator of the universe loves me more than I can imagine. Does that blow your mind too?

If you are having a hard time with love, I urge you to stop right now and ask God to show you what it is standing between you and love. Now, release it to Him. Maybe you don't feel lovely. Maybe you are walking around with a boat load of regret, shame and pain from your past. If the last statement describes you, this is what you need to do next. Sit down and make a list of every sin that is pulling you backwards. Then pray through each one and ask the Almighty to forgive you. Many times we don't allow ourselves to fully embrace God's love for us because we allow our past to haunt our present. However, once you have prayed through your past you can know your sin is COMPLETELY forgiven and gone from God's perspective forever.

Micah 7:18-19 (NIV) Who is a God like you, who pardons sin and forgives the transgression of the remnant of his inheritance? You do not stay angry forever but delight to show mercy. You will again have compassion on us; you will tread our sins underfoot and hurl all of our iniquities into the depths of the sea.

I love the study note under this scripture. It says, "God takes away sin's guilt so that it does not condemn us. He also takes away its power so that it does not rule over us." God totally takes our sin and any power it once held over us to the depths of the sea. If you feel as though you are not good enough to ask for forgiveness that is a lie from the enemy! Ask Jesus to reveal to you any issues you may have regarding accepting and experiencing His love. He will. He is faithful. God's love will change your life. The love of God can change any situation. Just believe. Like I said earlier – know for a fact nothing can separate you from the love of God. The Father's love is real and amazing – grab hold of it today. How? Start with this prayer. It is powerful stuff.

Ephesians 3:16–19 (NIV) I pray that out of His glorious riches He may strengthen you with power through His spirit in your inner being, so that Christ may dwell in your hearts through faith and I pray that you, being rooted and established in LOVE, may have power together with all the saints, to grasp how wide and long and high and deep is the LOVE of Christ and to know this LOVE that surpasses knowledge – that you may be filled to the measure of all the fullness of God.

I have prayed this prayer so many times for myself and others as well. Nothing will change you, as much as starting to understand the love which Jesus has for you. We will never be able to fully wrap our brains around it. By just attempting to understand this love you will change. Spiritual transformation – here we come!

Questions for thought...

    1) Are you struggling to love? Why?

    2) Do you understand in order to live the life God has planned for you – you must learn to love wholeheartedly?

    3) Are you ready to open your heart and experience a God sized love?

Action steps...

    Learning to love can be a difficult process, but not impossible. If your heart is behind a wall today take a look at *why*. Accept the fact that God's love can heal any and all hurts you've been hiding for years. He wants to heal your heart. Make a conscious effort to recognize when you shut down. In that moment, make another conscious effort to show love. It's one effort at a time which will begin to change your life.

Chapter 9

Discontentment

*S*itting on my couch staring at the wall with not one thought in my mind. I wasn't happy, something was missing but for the life of me I didn't know what it was. I quickly went through all of the positives in my life as if taking a test. Husband check, kids check, home check, car check, job check, so what was missing? Deep within me I longed for something. My soul was searching for something, just beyond my reach. This was me just months before my pastor more or less, dared me to read my Bible. I didn't know it at the time, but a deep seeded discontentment within me was the driving force toward Jesus.

According to Webster's Online Dictionary the definition of discontentment is *the condition of being dissatisfied with one's life situation*. Have you ever experience a day, a week, or longer when you were just not content? You can't seem to find *rest* in your mind. Discontentment can distance us from God or prod us in His direction. We want, what we want, when we want it; and if that doesn't work out, we are discontented. However, God's Word tells us there is a time for everything.

Ecclesiastes 3:1-8 (NIV) There is a time for everything, and a season for every activity under heaven: a time to be born and a time to die, a time to plan and a time to uproot, a time to kill and a time to heal, a time to tear down and a time to build, a time to weep and time to laugh, a time to mourn and a time to dance, a time to scatter stones and a time to gather them, a time to embrace and a time to refrain, a time to search and a time to give up, a time to keep and a time to throw away, a time to tear and a time to mend, a time to be silent and a time to speak, a time to love and a time to hate, a time for war and time for peace.

This scripture covers it all. God has a perfect time for everything. So, why do we waste our lives joyless? Why do we focus on the negative? Why are we discontented? For years, I was miserable. It was one of those unsettling emotions lying just under the surface that I could not put my finger on. I was just unhappy. I was in this state for so long, it became a habit or a way of life. It started to become difficult to imagine what it would *feel like* to live any other way. Do you feel that way?

I know discontentment from firsthand experience. It may start out with, "I'm unhappy in my marriage." This slowly grows into a general discontentment which seeps into every part of your life. Your job is not exactly what you want but it pays the bills. Your house provides a warm place to live but when you look around you see twenty repairs you would like to make, but you can't afford them. You look at your kids and you love them intensely but wonder if you are the best mother you can be. These are signs of a discontented heart. How you handle this heart is key.

Discontentment can be used to push us toward or pull us away from God. It becomes problematic when we wallow in it, and allow it to separate us from the Creator. Understanding where your discontentment is coming from is key to moving out of this state of mind.

Psalm 139:13 For you created my inmost being; you knit me together in my mother's womb.

Psalm 100:3 Know that the Lord is God. It is he who made us, and we are his; we are his people, the sheep of his pasture.

The truth really does set you free...

When I began to battle against discontentment I repeatedly reminded myself God created me and I was His. It was through this understanding that I started to find joy. As I read my Bible more and more I began to understand the misery I was in was self-perpetuated. God designed our inner beings. He designed us to feel emotions.

However, watch out, satan uses our emotions to persuade us into thinking our lives are hopeless. What a lie! I was stuck in extreme discontentment and convinced this was all my life was ever going to be. It troubles me today to even write those words. Over the last ten years the Almighty has given me a new found hope. He wants to give you that hope as well. I praise God each day for the unbelievable modifications He has made in me. I had no idea of the joy that was missing in my life. Remember, I started with a guarded heart and heaps of bitterness. God changed me, the one who began praying for only fifteen minutes each day just to prove her Pastor wrong.

Are you thinking, "Shari, you don't understand the circumstances in my life!" You're right I don't. God does. He has brought you here today for a reason and needs you to understand **in all circumstances** HE NEVER CHANGES. His love for you is real, passionate and eternal. He promises in His Word, He will never leave us or forsake us. This is who He is and this understanding changes us.

There was a time in my life when Bible reading felt like a chore; now it is pure joy. For months I begged God to grow an unquenchable desire deep within my soul for His Word. He did. I changed. I love the incredible stories in the Word because they were real then and hold real truth for us today. The God of Moses who parted the Red Sea is the same God who can transform your life forever. Think about it. The parting of the Red Sea was no small feat. Image yourself following Moses, your heart is racing, your mind is wondering and you come upon the Red Sea, a **gigantic** body of water. Are you thinking you made a mistake? Or, do you trust God for a miracle?

Exodus 14:21(NIV) Then Moses stretched out his hand over the sea, and all that night the Lord drove the sea back with a strong east wind and turned it into dry land. The waters were divided, and the Israelites went through the sea on dry ground, with a wall of water on their right and left.

Can you imagine this experience? Undoubtedly, the Israelites had lived a life of discontentment under Egyptian rule. Who would be happy living as a tortured slave? However, walking through the Red Sea, witnessing the wall of water all night must have been beyond comprehension! Just stop for a minute and try to visualize the miracle. It was God. He brought them out of bondage and into freedom. Yes, it did take them forty years, but once they started to understand obedience God was able to fulfill His promises.

Are you currently living in discontentment? Good news – the Almighty wants to give you hope and peace.

Psalm 118:5 (NIV) In my anguish I cried to the Lord, and he answered by setting me free.

Some practical how tos...

There is a freedom in God that took me a long time to understand. So many years I asked myself, "What does being free really look like?" The problem was who I was asking. Then, one day when I was praying over freedom the thought came to me. When was the last time I laughed? I mean really laughed out loud in a happy, knee-slapping belly laugh? Honestly, that day I could not remember. Next, I looked up the effects of laughter on the body and it turns out laughter is a great form of stress relief. Laughter is one of the best methods of emotional expression which allows our heart to be transformed from its current state of discontentment to relaxation. I know this may sound silly but I decided to be purposeful each day and look for something silly and laugh. I would like to challenge you to try this exercise. Find something to make you laugh–like a silly joke, a silly video on social media – anything, just laugh. It is hard to be grouchy while you are laughing. It was one of my first steps in moving out of habitual discontentment and into freedom.

How many times each day do you smile? Another part of my moving out of discontentment was to practice smiling. I know this sounds silly too, but you'll be surprised at the change in your outlook and those around you. Smile. You may not even be aware you don't smile much until you stop and think about it. You are a beloved daughter of the King and I bet if you think long enough you will find at least one thing in your life that will put a smile on your face. Now let's revisit Ephesians for this powerful prayer.

Ephesians 3:16-19 (NIV) I pray that out of his glorious riches he may strengthen you with power through His spirit in your inner being, so that Christ may dwell in your hearts through faith. And I pray that you, being rooted and established in love, may have power, together with all the saints, to grasp how wide and long and high and deep in the love of Christ, and to know this love that surpasses knowledge – that you may be filled to the measure of the fullness of God.

Read this prayer again and this time make it personal…

Ephesians 3:16-19 (NIV) I pray that out of His glorious riches He may strengthen me with power through His spirit in my inner being, so that Christ may dwell in my heart through faith. And I pray that Shari, being rooted and established in love, may have power, together with all the saints, to grasp how wide and long and high and deep in the love of Christ, and to know this love that surpasses knowledge – that I may be filled to the measure of the fullness of God.

As the truth of God's Word penetrates your mind, the chains of discontentment will begin to loosen. Allow yourself to see through the eyes and heart of Jesus.

Questions for thought...

1) Are you discontented with your life?

2) Can you identify what in your life are you discontented with?

3) Can you honestly say you are ready to move out of this season of your life?

Action steps...

Often discontentment comes when we are looking for something new in our lives. God wants to be your something new today. I know the suggestions of laughing and smiling may seem silly but some small practical steps can start you in the right direction. Take some time each day to focus on the positive and look for signs of God all around you.

Chapter 10

When I was younger one of my favorite things to do was to go the mall and watch people. I could happily sit for an hour and just watch all the people go by. However, while watching it was easy to categorize people. He's rich, she's beautiful, he's domineering, and she's just plain snooty. Sad to say, but that was how I used to think. How about you? The truth is that judging others is God's job not ours.

Romans 2:1 (NIV) You, therefore, have no excuses, you who pass judgment on someone else, for at whatever point you judge the other you are condemning yourself, because you who pass judgment do the same things. Now we know that God's judgment against those who do such things is based on truth. So when you, a mere man, pass judgment on them and yet do the same things, do you think you will escape God's judgment?

The Word is exceedingly clear. We are all sinners and all sin. However, if we choose in our heart to judge someone–we are actually asking for God's judgment in our own lives. Are you ready for that?

Love covers a multitude of sin...

Fourteen years ago I was sitting in a Pediatrician's office waiting for the nurse to call my daughter's name when this little boy and his mom walked through the door. Their clothes were dirty. I automatically found myself hoping he did not want to come over and play with my daughter. I automatically started thinking, "Why doesn't she take better care of that kid?" I automatically started judging. Does this sound familiar? It was where I was then and it may be where you are today. I didn't think I was a judgmental person it was just automatic. This thought process is actually the opposite of what Jesus calls us to.

1 Peter 4:8 (NIV) Above all, love each other deeply, because love covers over a multitude of sins. (Love forgives again and again....)

Love covers a multitude of sin. Sin is sin. God does not grade sin on a scale of one to ten. In His eyes, it is all the same–sin. God's viewpoint at times is hard to understand and that is okay. We will never truly understand the Lord's perception of life until we have the opportunity to ask Him directly. If you tell a lie, it's a sin. If you want your neighbor's new car so bad it bothers you, it's a sin. If you kill someone, it's a sin. If you get drunk, it's a sin. It's all the same in God's eyes. It's wrong.

Romans 2:11(NIV) For God does not show favoritism. All who sin apart from the law will also perish apart from the law, and all who sin under the law will be judged by the law. For it is not those who hear the law who are righteous in God's sight, but it is those who obey the law who will be declared righteous.

Having God call me righteous some day is far more important than being right on earth. In other words, I have given up my fleshy desire to be right. I deeply desire to follow God's Word. So, sitting in that doctor's office fourteen years ago I found myself with a cold heart and a judgmental mind. What about you? Do you harbor some secret judgment against someone? Remember satan knows what button to push to lead you into sin and he will push it daily **if allowed**. It's not about the clothes we wear, the cars we drive or the homes we live in. The truth is, it is about loving, giving and keeping your heart pure and your mind clean. My husband's grandmother always said "garbage in, garbage out." This is so simple yet so true. If you allow sinful thoughts to enter your mind, like thoughts of judgment and condemnation, you will end up on sin's doorstep. It's inevitable.

Train your brain to stay in the positive zone. When a negative thought enters your mind, immediately recognize it for what it is.

Think of one of your favorite scripture verses and ask God to remove it from your mind. If you allow judgmental thoughts in your brain, they automatically seep into your heart–that's how the sin becomes extremely toxic and poisons your spiritual walk.

Romans 8:5-8 (NIV) Those who live according to the sinful nature have their minds set on what that nature desires; but those who live in accordance with the Spirit have their minds set on what the Spirit desires. The mind of a sinful man is death, but the mind controlled by the Spirit is life and peace; a sinful mind is hostile to God. It does not submit to God's law nor can it do so. Those controlled by the sinful nature cannot please God.

Sin whatever the form is not pleasing to the Lord. Minds which are controlled by sin are hostile to God. The last thing I want is our Heavenly Father to view me as hostile in His sight. How about you? Take a few minutes and say this prayer with me...

Dear God, I ask you to show me any judgments I have made in my mind or in my heart against another. I ask you to reveal these to me so I may repent and dissolve this sin in my life. I want nothing more than to serve you and rid myself of anything distasteful and ungodly. Forgive me Father and replace this sin with your love; the true love of God which forgives again and again, in Jesus name, Amen.

Don't be afraid to pray this prayer over and over until it soaks into your spirit.

Questions for thought...

1) Do you find yourself judging other, sometimes without even thinking about it?

2) Do you feel the need to make comparisons with others?

3) Are you ready to lay your judgement of others aside?

Action Steps...

Train your brain. Whenever you begin to judge someone stop the thought process before it has time to grow. Remind yourself, God is the only judge and this line of thinking is truly a waste of time.

Chapter 11

Anger & Jealousy

*I*t was my twenty-first birthday and my husband decided to surprise me with two tickets to a concert of one of my favorite artists. I was thrilled! We had only been married for a couple of months and this event would set the bar for birthdays. I spent hours going through my closet searching for the perfect outfit. On the drive to the concert, I kept telling him how excited I was and how wonderful this evening was going to be. My husband invited his college buddies to the concert. When we arrived we met them for a drink. One drink turned into several for each of the guys and I was beginning to think this was more of a party for him than me. We went into the concert and found our seats. The lights dimmed, the music started and I began to forget about the excessive drinking and focus on the artists. It wasn't long until one of our invited guests left and return with more drinks. As he was passing my husband a full beer it accidentally spilled on the gentleman's wife in front of us. The guy stood up and I started to apologize immediately. Nevertheless, insults between two drunk men quickly got underway. Words escalated into pushing until another guy and myself were trapped between them like sardines. I grabbed my husband's face and screamed "STOP IT" at the top of my lungs. He sat back down. The evening was ruined, my heart broken and the thought of "did I make a mistake?" lingered in my mind.

In your anger, don't sin…

Anger is an emotion we have all experienced at one time or another. It is unrealistic to think we will never become angry. The point is, when we are angry, how do we handle it?

Ephesians 4: 26-27 (NIV) In your anger do not sin. Do not let the sun go down while you are still angry, and do not give the Devil a foothold."

James 1: 19–20 (NIV) My dear brothers, take note of this: everyone should be quick to listen, slow to speak and slow to become angry, for man's anger does not bring about the righteous life that God desires.

Scripture does not tell us to not become angry. Instead, we are told to be slow to anger and when we are angry, careful not to sin. What exactly does that behavioral pattern look like in life? Let's say someone is talking about you, how do you handle it? It's acceptable to become angry when you are wronged. The key is what do you do about it? Do you call the person and give them a piece of your mind? Do you pray for them and ask God to help you forgive and love them? It takes time to come down after an *angry high*. However, it is the end result God wants.

If your kids or husband leave their clothes on the floor rather than in the hamper do you get irritated? Yes, we all do if we are honest. When you are mad, how do you handle it? Are you a screamer, thrower or slammer? Do you have control or do you lose control? I can talk about anger because I used to deal with it on a daily basis. Looking back, it was like a friend to me. Anger was familiar and I could count on him to visit me multiple times each week and sometimes even each day. When I would get annoyed, I would yell. I think at times I actually enjoyed yelling because it was such a relief. I know from experience all yelling does is hurt the recipients with words that can never be taken back.

For me, showing my anger was easier than dealing with the real issue–which was discontentment. I used anger as a way to avoid the actual problem. I am being blunt about my own experiences in order for you to understand that we all go through difficult times in our lives. We all suffer and hurt others. Once you've decided only Jesus can deal with your anger, He gladly will. You've heard people say "when life gives you lemons make lemonade" – the picture of Jesus wringing out our sour parts, is a visual I love. The point is, it doesn't matter how angry you are, God can deal with it. He was the one who created you and He holds the master key to your soul. Don't let the enemy convince you surrendering to God is impossible. That's a lie. The moment you give God your anger it can't hurt you or anyone else once.

Remember, Jesus died for your sins, so you don't have to carry them around in one big ball of anger. The enemy is crafty and will fill your mind with negative scenarios to keep you spinning in a pit of anger. Still, you must remember the Almighty created you and longs for you each moment of each day. God designed us and He made anger a part of us. He also gave us His Word in order to understand how to deal with it.

The most effective action you can take when you are angry is to pray for the person and/or situation that angered you. **I know** it is not an easy thing to do. Sometimes you may need to go and scream into a pillow first. I used to enjoy this exercise regularly. However, the peace you will receive once you begin to deal with your anger in a Godly way is priceless. Let's be honest, nine times out of ten the one who angered you is not even aware or upset about the issue, it is just you.

Romans 12:19-21 (NIV) Do not take revenge, my friends, but leave room for God's wrath, for it is written: "It is mine to avenge; I will repay," says the Lord. On the contrary, "If your enemy is hungry, feed him; if he is thirsty, give him something to drink. In doing this, you will heap burning coals on his head. Do not be overcomed by evil, but overcome evil with good.

I have witnessed first-hand the difference in me trying to deal with my anger and me allowing God to deal with my anger. Here's a perfect example. I have been employed by a local church for almost ten years as a Worship Leader. I have a team of twenty amazing people and one of my spiritual gifts is administration so I am organized. Over the past ten years the church has expanded from sixty to four hundred and accompaniment CDs to a full band. Several years ago our church was experiencing turmoil. During this time, the Pastor and I did not always agree on many things.

One day the Pastor told me he was thinking perhaps our church needed a change. Maybe what we needed was a twenty year old male with ripped jeans leading worship rather than a fortyish female. My first reaction was anger, the kind where your blood boils in a matter of seconds. I had visions of me throat punching him instantly. I told you, I had anger issues. I just walked away.

I was determined to see if this was a God thing, a Pastor thing or a me thing. So I began to pray. For three months I met with God each morning on my back porch, read scripture and prayed feverishly over what I should do and how to release this gut wrenching anger inside of me. I came to the conclusion I needed to submit. I was going offer my resignation. If he wanted a male worship leader then so be it. If this was what God was telling him, even though I had still not received that message from God, I needed to be obedient to the authority placed over me and resign. I scheduled an appointment and started off with "I've been praying about this for the last three months and I'm okay if the direction you feel the church needs to take is for a young man to step in so I'm giving you my resignation." The color left his face. At that moment, exactly the opposite of what I expected to happen, happened. He said the Holy Spirit had convicted him that changing worship leaders was not the best direction for the church. He went on to say the problem was in our relationship or the lack thereof. I agreed. That day I began to see him through the eyes of Jesus. He is a man, and men make mistakes, even Pastors. Nevertheless, I am blessed to serve under a man who loves the Lord with all of his heart and wants nothing more than to spread the Word of God to all nations. This Pastor is the one who first challenged me to read my Bible for fifteen minutes each day and who I have grown-up spiritually under for the past ten years. Needless to say the love and gratitude I have for him is genuine.

If I had chosen to deal with the anger myself, I'm sure this story would have a different ending. You see ladies only God can give us the best outcomes to our anger. It is up to us to be obedient and give it to Him to deal with. I know it is difficult to surrender your anger to the Lord, however, He can and will work the situation out better than you ever could. Just trust Him.

Jealousy – the green eyed monster...

Now, let's talk about jealousy. Jealousy can take several forms. One of the first that comes to mind is in the male/female relationship. However, if you are over the age of 40 your jealousy may have nothing to do with the opposite sex. God has some specific thoughts on the topic.....

Deuteronomy 5:21 (NIV) You shall not covet your neighbor's wife. You shall not set your desire on your neighbor's house or land, his manservant or maidservant, his ox or donkey or anything that belongs to your neighbor."

The Bible is straight forward on this topic. We are not to be jealous of people for what they have or who they are with. Sin comes in when we dwell on what others have that we do not. This world we live in is only our temporary home. If the world exploded tomorrow would anyone care what your house looked like?

Think about it. At the end of the day does it really matter if our throw pillows cost $5 or $50? The world of advertising conveys we need the best of everything. You see the key is to line up our perceptions with the Word of God. We must fix our eyes on Jesus, our eternal home and ignore the lusts of this world.

How much time do you spend on social media or surfing the web? It is easy to lose track of time just looking at all of the attractions of the world. The key is not to allow yourself to focus on what others have. I know at times this is easier said than done and can happen without you being consciously aware of it. God knew that too.

2 Corinthians 10:5 (NIV) We demolish arguments and every pretension that sets itself up against the knowledge of God, and we take captive every thought to make it obedient to Christ.

Here is a battle plan for when your mind wanders. Take the thought and line it up with the Word of God. We are called to take **every thought** which flows through our brain captive and make it obedient to Christ. This takes practice, practice, practice! You can't make your thoughts obedient to Christ if you don't know what the

Bible says about Him. I repeat this point because it is absolutely imperative for your growth in Jesus. You must first be mentally aware of your thoughts. Just try it. Keeping your mind in a positive state can become a habit – a righteous habit which will transform your life. When do I start, you ask? Today, right now. From this moment on when something negative pops into your mind, push in out with "God, please give me the mind of Jesus." This simple prayer can drive out the undesirable thoughts and change your focus.

It may sound strange, but the more you practice taking control of your thoughts and keeping them in a good place, the easier it becomes and before you know it, it is your normal.

Questions for thought…

1) Do you struggle with anger? What makes you angry?

2) Do you struggle with jealousy?

3) Are you ready to begin some spiritual work in these areas?

Action steps…

If you recognize that anger and jealousy are problems for you, that's the first step. When you are angry, walk away and process with God. When thoughts of jealousy come forward in your mind – push them out with scripture. Remember it is better to keep your mouth closed than to verbally vomit on others.

Chapter 12

Peace & Joy

I was waiting anxiously for an update on a friend's health who was in the hospital. She had been severely ill and lingering between life and death for several days. I believe God heals. I do not know why He chooses who He chooses to heal but I know, He does. After several hours of looking at my phone to see if I missed a text I decided to message another friend for an update. Finally, the update came. Nothing had changed in the last twenty-four hours. I immediately tensed up and started to plead with God. Almost instantly I was overtaken with a peace that settled every nerve in my body. A peace that allowed me to breathe freely and dried up my tears. God whispered to my soul, my friend would recover and I had nothing to fear. I experienced the peace of the Almighty. Peace that flowed over me like warm rays of sunshine after a long winter. It was God.

Have you ever experienced that peace? What does peace mean to you? Each one of us may have some variation of what peace looks like in our life. Basically peace means being calm and quiet, **with no anxiety**. I understand this may be a difficult concept for some but this peace is available to all.

Philippians 4:6-7 (NIV) Do not be anxious about anything, but in everything, by prayer and petition, with thanksgiving, present your requests to God. And the peace of God, which transcends all understanding, will guard your hearts and your minds in Christ Jesus.

Let's examine this scripture. God created all things and knows all things. God views everything through the lens of victory. Why? Because He knows the end of the story and so do we. He is victorious over the enemy, and a heavenly eternity awaits those who love and follow Him. Seriously, I'm not sure I am humanly capable to fully understand what the word "peace" means to God. Can you imagine how different your life would be if you filtered every thought through the lens of **victory**? This is what the NIV Study Bible says regarding this passage:

peace of God. Not merely a psychological state of mind, but an inner tranquility based on peace with God – the peaceful state of those whose sins are forgiven. The opposite of anxiety, it is the tranquility that comes when believers commit all their cares to God in prayer and worry about them no more.

transcends all understanding. The full dimensions of God's love and care are beyond human comprehension.

guard….hearts…minds…. A military concept depicting a soldier standing guard. God's protective custody of those who are in Christ Jesus extends to the **core of their beings and to their deepest intentions.**

First the peace described here is opposite of anxiety. In this peace there are no "what ifs" floating around in our minds. Next, we are reminded that the way we are loved and cared for is beyond our comprehension. WOW! The next part of the explanation tells us God's protective custody extends to our very core and deepest intentions. We are deeply loved as the Creator's children. This love is much more than we will ever be able to comprehend here on earth. Just think about that! We are blessed to have God's peace to guard us. The exact body part satan is constantly trying to attack – your mind – is guarded by God! You have HIS PEACE which nothing can take away from you. We must fully accept this concept. We have God's "protective custody" in the core of our very being. Stop and think about this for a moment because it is enormous. I want you to completely understand what this means to you personally, as a daughter of the King. This means no matter what you are facing in life, you have God's peace in your core being, and **nothing can destroy that.**

You and I can have this astounding peace which we don't even understand. So, why aren't you living in it?

God's ways are always higher...

It was my husband's fortieth birthday and I spent the entire day trying to make his birthday just perfect. I decorated the house with balloons, signs and ribbon. I made his favorite dish for dinner, picked up his favorite cake and ice cream and bought a few presents for him to open. He spent the morning hunting (one of his favorite things) and then came home for a nap. I was excited to make this day special for him. However, he informed me he was going to go out for a few hours with the boys and would not be home until 6:30 pm. I countered with "but I have worship practice tonight so could we make dinner a little earlier?" He said "Okay, I'll be home by 6:00 pm." It was 5:55 pm and he still was not home. The food was in the oven just to keep warm. I called and he said he was just leaving and should be home in another twenty minutes. I was furious! I could not believe I went to all of this trouble! The least he could do was to show up for his birthday dinner. I was somewhat short on the phone as I felt my face turning red with anger. My eyes welled up with tears and off to my favorite place (my bathroom) I ran. This event occurred the year I was working on submission. As soon as the door closed behind me I started screaming at God.

First, I was livid at my husband for not being home on time and hurting my feelings. Second, I was furious at God because He allowed this to happen to me. I mean come on–it wasn't that long ago He deflated the rubber ball around my heart. All I wanted was to serve Him. Why would He allow me to experience such pain? Well, Jesus let me blubber for a few minutes and then He said very clearly, "Your ways are not my ways." I said, "What?" He further informed me I was human and did not possess the capacity to love the way I was called to without His supernatural touch. I again cried out, "then it's not in me, I can't just let go, Lord, I need you to do something right now!" At that very moment a peace, which totally transcended all of my understanding, the one I described earlier in this chapter, came over me. Honestly, I was no longer hurting or angry. It was strange. I was filled with love and peace. I was taken back at first because I knew right away this was God, front and center. This was real.

You see, I had been struggling with understanding how to show God's love in my life, especially in my home. The Lord showed up when I called and within minutes He filled me with His love and peace. There was no room in my heart or my mind for anything else. I was able to greet my husband cheerfully when he arrived and could smile, really smile (with love from my soul) all during dinner and the rest of the evening.

I will never forget God's faithfulness he showered on me that day. He showed me firsthand what He expects of me. The love and forgiveness that I don't always possess are just a request away. This is totally opposite ladies of self-help. This is Jesus help and it is the **only way** for permanent, lasting change in our lives. His ways are not my ways. But, I want them to be. The only way to get there is to constantly seek Him and ASK.

God is waiting to fill you, too. As Christians, we are still going to encounter problems and tough times. But, with God all things are bearable; He provides as long as you seek. This was an example of immediate peace in a desperate situation. Just think about what could have happened if I had not cried out to God. I'm sure when my husband came home I would have been angry and ruined his fortieth birthday. It would have been an event he remembered for the rest of his life.

One thing I remind myself of on a regular basis is that God provides His peace not only in moments of chaos but every day.

1 Thessalonians 5:16 (NIV) Be joyful always; pray continually; give thanks in all circumstances, for this is God's will for you in Christ Jesus.

This is specific direction from God's Word. Hard? Sometimes, but not impossible. How do you enter into God's peace and joy? I know you may be thinking "Sister you have no idea what I live with." You are right I don't, I would never pretend to, Jesus does and He wants desperately to be Lord in your home.

Get to know Him by praying and reading His Word. As your relationship with Jesus grows, so will your peace and joy. You will change. What was once important (like the latest fashion, always being right, a new car or holding on to anger) no longer has any merit in your life because you are focused on following Jesus.

Are you full of anxiety, stress and worry? Then, what are you waiting on? Dig into the Word of God and allow the truth to change your perspective. Knowing God is truly knowing peace.

Questions for thought...

1) Are you struggling with the lack of peace in your life?

2) Are you seeking and not finding at the moment?

3) Are you ready to try something new to discover God's promised peace?

Action steps...

A big part of finding peace is having a mind and heart knowledge that you are really not in control–God is. It is also recognizing that He will never leave you. Repeat *God will never leave me*, until it is firm within your soul. Now give God the freedom to be Lord in your home.

Chapter 13

Royalty

*H*ow does it feel to be the daughter of the most-high God? Do you realize once you accept Christ as your personal Savior that is your title? First, let's look at scripture for complete clarification.

Romans 8:15 – 17 (NIV) For you did not receive a spirit that makes you a slave again to fear, but you received the Spirit of sonship. And by him we cry, Abba, Father. The Spirit himself testifies with our spirit that we are God's children. Now if we are children, then we are heirs – heirs of God and co-heirs with Christ, if indeed we share in his sufferings in order that we may also share in his glory.

Let's break this down. Those who receive the spirit (ask the Holy Spirit to come and live inside them) are co-heirs with Jesus as sons and daughters of God. That is huge! I don't know about you, but calling me a co-heir with Jesus can be a little overwhelming. However, that is exactly what the Word teaches us, does it not? Our Father God loves us so much that He refers to us as "co-heirs with Christ."

Let's focus on the first part of this scripture. The Word tells us the Holy Spirit living inside of us frees us from fear. That is a God promise Sister! Are you dealing with issues of fear? The enemy loves to use fear to hold us captive. However, the Creator of the Universe is our Dad so what REALLY do we have to be afraid of?

When I first became serious about growing in Jesus I immediately remembered my past and many things I now deeply regretted. I was struggling with my past sin and needed desperately to give it to The Savior. I decided to write down all of the sins that were holding me captive and pray through each one asking God to forgive me. I started with sins of my teenage years and prayed all the way through present day. This took some time, however, with tears of release I confessed each sin before my Savior, repented and moved on to the next one. By the end of my prayer time, my shirt was soaked with tears, but my heart was the lightest it had ever been. God showed me how He saw me. Needless to say, I cried even harder. Jesus sees the best in us. He sees His creation with nothing but love. When God looks at you, He views a daughter deeply loved and one He cannot wait to welcome home. Think about it. How do you see people you love? When you look at them do you see all of their flaws or do you see the beauty inside? The same is true with our Father. When He looks at us, He sees love.

You really are a princess…

Let's think about royalty for a minute. When you think of royalty, does your mind automatically go to palaces and crowns? Can we as common folk comprehend the mindset of those in royal positions? If you see someone hungry do you buy them a meal? Ask a generous king for food and he may give you a farm with fields of planted vegetables, along with all of the livestock you would need to fully sustain your family. If someone told you they had a car problem, you may offer them a ride to where they needed to go. If someone told a king they had a car problem he may give them a new car or even several of their choosing. You see, royalty thinks differently and that is just an earthly example. Just imagine how much more your Father in Heaven wants to give you, wants to tell you, and wants to show you. Most of us do not think like royalty but God does and beyond earthly comprehension. So, if we are co-heirs with Jesus, why do we still live in fear? If we are co-heirs with Jesus, why are we not loving others? If we are co-heirs with Jesus, why are we still angry all of the time? We should know that our Father, the Almighty, can take care of whatever arises in our lives and allow this truth to give us peace, joy and love.

Galatians 4:6-7 (NIV) Because you are sons, God sent the Spirit of his Son into your hearts, the Spirit who calls out, Abba, Father. So you are no longer a slave, but a son; and since you are a son, God has made you also an heir.

Do you think a princess fears she will not have everything she needs? No – she doesn't even give it a second thought. God is right here, right now. He is ready to take care of your every need, every day if you will only allow him to be Abba, Father. What does this exactly mean, you ask? It means, read your Bible each day. Pray each day, look for God and you will find Him face to face. He will take care of your every need, and many things He will do even before you ask or the need arises.

Hebrews 1:1-4 (NIV) In the past God spoke to our forefathers through the prophets at many times and in various ways, but in these last days he has spoken to us by his Son, whom he appointed heir of all things, and through whom he made the universe. The Son is the radiance of God's glory and the exact representation of his being, sustaining all things by his powerful word. After he had provided purification for sins, he sat down at the right hand of the Majesty in heaven. So he became as much superior to the angels as the name he has inherited is superior to theirs.

Again, stop and re-read this passage. It is mammoth in helping us see how daughters of the King should look. We are called to be the "radiance of God's glory and the exact representation of His being, sustaining all things by His powerful word." Think about that for a few minutes. We are to show the world who we belong to by trying to live each day with God leading us. We can do these things because we have the Holy Spirit living in us and we have the Word guiding us. If you are not in the Word of God each day, you are going to have a hard time growing spiritually. It's impossible to be the Word if you don't know the Word. Allow God's Word to penetrate your heart each day. Pray that God will open your heart to hear the message of His word each day. As children of the King we have confidence that God is in charge of our lives. We know that no matter what happens Jesus will never leave His children. He will love us more than we can ever imagine. As long as we seek Him, we will not be disappointed.

I'm from the South and one of things I think of from my child-hood is *being spoiled rotten*. Do you know what I mean? My mother was one of one of thirteen children and my Grandmother had a ton of Grandchildren. Holiday dinners at Grandmas always meant you would meet a new cousin. However, my Grandparents spoiled me. I'll never forget one special night when Grandma led me into her bedroom and had me look under the bed and there was this big flat box with a bow on it. The excitement in the room at that moment could have literally blew the roof off. I could not believe it was for me. I carefully pulled it from under the bed and untied the bow. There was a beautiful dress just for me. I was elated! Next my Granddad came in and said, "Little lady after supper you want to go get some ice cream?" Who would EVER say "no" to that?! My Grandparents spoiled me rotten. Not only with gifts but by showing me that I was loved. Ladies, this is exactly what our Heavenly Father has for each one of us. He wants to spoil us rotten.

Psalm 37:4 (NIV) Take delight in the Lord, and he will give you the desires of your heart.

What are the desires of your heart? No matter how big or how small He wants to give those to you. The biggest desire of my heart was for my entire family to serve Him. Ladies it takes work to train up your children. To allow those around you to see God's love flowing from your actions and words. It takes patience as you allow God to work on your husband or best friend and you keep your hands off. However, the rewards are unimaginable. Are you ready to be *spoiled rotten* by the Creator of the Universe? He may not do everything the way you want or at the time you want Him to – but He will provide everything you need in His time.

Questions for thought...

1) Are you holding onto any guilt that is keeping you from seeing yourself as a daughter of the King?

2) What are the desires of your heart?

3) Are you ready to accept your place of royalty?

Action steps...

If you are holding onto past sins, write them down and pray through your list. Once you are finished you must understand that God not only forgave them but erased them from His memory. You are free from those sins and they have no power over you anymore. Now look at yourself in the mirror and see the beauty that God sees.

Chapter 14

Freedom

*W*hat does it really mean to be free? Webster's dictionary defines freedom as- *the power to act, think or speak without externally imposed restraints*. Let's think about this in a spiritual sense – what is spiritually restraining you from freedom?

Have you ever been deeply hurt by someone? Most of us have. Forgiveness is a basic scriptural principle. It is what we seek from our Father God on a daily basis and what He calls us to give freely to each other. The Bible clearly states God's view of forgiveness. A beautiful example of forgiveness can be found in the stories of the people God chose to carry out His plan: Jacob was insecure, Rahab was immoral, David had an affair and family problems, Elijah was suicidal, Martha worried, and Peter denied he even knew Jesus. God forgave them and used them in a mighty ways.

Isaiah 38:17 (NIV) Surely it was for my benefit that I suffered such anguish. In your love you kept me from the pit of destruction; you have put all my sins behind your back.

The NIV note says, "God not only puts our sins out of sight, He also puts them out of reach, out of mind and out of existence."

God not only forgives our sins, He puts them out of His mind and completely out of existence. How can we see ourselves as hopeless when God doesn't even remember our sins once we ask for forgiveness? **Sometimes the lack of our understanding of our own forgiveness can be the restraint.** Have you fully accepted that the Creator of the Universe has forgiven **and** forgotten all of your sins, the moment you asked Him to?

Jesus showed me the only way to truly be free was to honestly accept who I am in Him. I am a sinner who was saved by the grace of God and the blood of Jesus Christ. I am forgiven, loved and held close to my Father's heart. If you have accepted Jesus as your personal Lord and Savior then Sister the same is true for you.

We must fully accept God's grace and our personal redemption— before we can ever truly be free. In order to live our lives in God's freedom, we must first forgive ourselves, recognize that we are full-blooded daughters of Christ and forgive those who have hurt us. You must believe the Word of God is truth and know when Jesus looks at you, He sees you through eyes of love.

You are valued...

For the longest time when I first started seeking Jesus, I did not see myself how He saw me. Therefore, I was not living in true freedom. My biggest issue was letting go of anger and loving. God slowly freed me by melting the rubber walls around my heart. Don't get me wrong, I still get angry from time to time. Now I can control my actions and my words, and give God time to process with me rather than blowing up everyone in my path. Praise God – He set me free! He can set you free too. Let's take a look at some scripture to back up my claim:

Acts 13:38-39(NIV) Therefore my brothers, I want you to know that through Jesus the forgiveness of sins is proclaimed to you. Through Him everyone who believes is justified from everything you could not be justified from by the Law of Moses.

NIV Notes: Justification combines two aspects 1) the forgiveness of sins and 2) the gift of righteousness.

Micah 7:18-19 (NIV) Who is a God like you, who pardons sin and forgives the transgression of the remnant of his inheritance? You do not stay angry forever but delight to show mercy. You will again have compassion on us; you will tread our sins underfoot and hurl all our iniquities into the depths of the sea.

To live in freedom you must completely accept not just your forgiveness from Jesus but also the gift of righteousness which He graciously administers in the forgiveness process. Until you begin to see yourself the way God sees you, you will never truly taste authentic freedom. So let's give it a try. I want you to see yourself at your best. Your hair is perfect, your makeup is flawless, your body is exactly what you want it to be, but most important there is a purity about your soul. This purity becomes visual as a *radiance of righteousness* which sparkles all around you. Close your eyes and see it. I like to think this is how God sees us. Our souls sparkle before our Lord and we are at our finest.

Do you know how valuable you are? God views you as a beloved daughter and nothing less. Once you accept this truth, it will change the way you see yourself. Meditate on this truth until your soul absorbs it. Remember you sparkle! It IS who you are now. You will make mistakes, you will never be perfect. However, your Father in Heaven already knows that.

Finally, if you have any unforgiven hurts that you have been holding onto, pray through them and forgive those who hurt you. How can we stand before the Almighty each day and ask Him to forgive us when we are harboring unforgiveness toward someone else. This may take some time as well. That's okay! Our growth in Jesus is a marathon not a sprint. Just stick with it. Stay the course.

It is my prayer that while reading this book something has touched your spirit and changed within you. If you don't go to church, find one that teaches the Bible. Connect with other women who also love the Lord and dig into growing in Christ with others. God has some big plans for your life! So what are you waiting for?

Questions for thought...

1) Are you living in freedom today? If no, why?

2) Are you struggling with self-doubt? Why?

3) Are you ready to move forward with God?

Action steps...

Jesus went to the cross to give us the freedom the Bible is full of. When we do not fully step into that freedom each day we are robbing the cross of that amazing power. Not to mention living only a lukewarm life. You are fully forgiven, loved, saved, called out and chosen. As a daughter of the Creator allow the truths of who you are to penetrate your mind and heart.

Closing Comments

*I*t is my prayer the words you've read in this book have opened your eyes to look at Jesus differently. Trust me, if any "light bulbs" went off while reading this book it is because of God, not me.

Again I say this is my story and I wrote this some seven years ago and recently pulled it out, gave it a good editing and put it out there. Please don't ever judge yourself or your spirituality based on others. God calls us to live in relationship with Him. Your walk with Jesus will look different than mine. The God we serve is bigger than we can ever imagine, so don't put Him in a box. Don't limit Him. Live your life the way God intended; focused on your eternal rewards. Strive each day to know Him more. Seek His face daily and love as much as you possibly can, together as the body of Christ, we can change the world. You CAN DO THIS!

CPSIA information can be obtained
at www.ICGtesting.com
Printed in the USA
FFOW05n0744210116

9 781498 453349